WORKBOOK

English 1
Explorer

Jane Bailey
with Helen Stephenson

Australia • Brazil • Japan • Korea • Mexico • Singapore • Spain • United Kingdom • United States

English Explorer Workbook 1
Jane Bailey with Helen Stephenson

Publisher: Jason Mann

Adaptations Manager: Alistair Baxter

Assistant Editor: Manuela Barros

Product and Marketing Manager:
   Ruth McAleavey

Senior Content Project Editor: Natalie Griffith

Senior Production Controller: Paul Herbert

National Geographic Liaison: Leila Hishmeh

Cover Designer: Natasa Arsenidou

Text Designer: eMC Design Ltd., UK and
   PreMedia Global

Compositor: PreMedia Global

Audio: EFS Television Production Ltd.

Acknowledgments
The Publisher would like to thank the following for
their invaluable contribution: Nick Sheard, Karen
Spiller and Karen Chambers.

ISBN: 978-1-111-05525-7

National Geographic Learning
Cheriton House, North Way, Andover, Hampshire, SP10 5BE
United Kingdom

Cengage Learning is a leading provider of customized learning solutions with
office locations around the globe, including Singapore, the United Kingdom,
Australia, Mexico, Brazil and Japan. Locate your local office at:
international.cengage.com/region

Cengage Learning products are represented in Canada
by Nelson Education, Ltd.

Visit National Geographic Learning online at **ngl.cengage.com**

Visit our corporate website at **www.cengage.com**

Photo credits

The publishers would like to thank the following sources for permission to reproduce their copyright protected photographs:

Cover photo: Alaska Stock Images / National Geographic Image Collection

6 (Rob Byron – Fotolia.com), 12 (Galina Barskaya – Fotolia.com), 14t (Shutterstock.com), 14b (eurobanks/iStockphoto.com), 15 (Michael Nichols/National Geographic Image Collection), 18 1 (charles taylor – Fotolia.com), 18 2 (amorphis – Fotolia.com), 18 3 (Sebastian Duda – Fotolia.com), 18 4 (Vadim Andrushchenko – Fotolia.com), 18 5 (aberenyi – Fotolia.com), 18 6 (ygrek – Fotolia.com), 18 7 (volkanersoy – Fotolia.com), 18 8 (Kent Christopherson. Image from BigStockPhoto.com), 19 (mg7. Image from BigStockPhoto.com), 20tr (EastWestImaging. Image from BigStockPhoto.com), 20tl (Perkmeup. Image from BigStockPhoto.com), 20l (lilly3/iStockphoto.com), 20br (N M – Fotolia.com), 21 (ITV/Rex Features), 23 (wdstock/iStockphoto.com), 25 stamp (alverdissen. Image from BigStockPhoto.com), 25c (PinkTag/iStockphoto.com), 25b (Hagrit/iStockphoto.com), 30ta (winterberg. Image from BigStockPhoto.com), 30tb (slovegrove. Image from BigStockPhoto.com), 30tc (Galina Barskaya – Fotolia.com), 30td (Elena Elisseeva – Fotolia.com), 30te (Graça Victoria/123rf.com), 30tf (gvictoria. Image from BigStockPhoto.com), 30tg (Igor Gromoff – Fotolia.com), 30th (Ted Streshinsky/Corbis), 30ba (Tatyana Nyshko – Fotolia.com), 30bc (Andrzej Puchta – Fotolia.com), 30bd (BVDC – Fotolia.com), 30be (AndersonRise – Fotolia.com), 30bf (TheSupe87 – Fotolia.com), 32a (John Green/BEI/Rex Features), 32b (Norm Betts/Rex Features), 32c (Picture Perfect/Rex Features), 33l (mrslevite – Fotolia.com), 33r (Maridav – Fotolia.com), 34l (Alx – Fotolia.com), 34cl (Andre – Fotolia.com), 34cr (robynmac – Fotolia.com), 34r (elvinstar. Image from BigStockPhoto.com), 35 (Liv Friis-larsen – Fotolia.com), 36a (bc173/iStockphoto.com), 36b (Photodisc/Alamy), 36c (Shutterstock.com), 36d (David Mzareulyan/Shutterstock, Inc), 36e (Yuri Arcurs/123rf.com), 37a (elli – Fotolia.com), 37b (victorburnside. Image from BigStockPhoto.com), 37c (monkeybusinessimages. Image from BigStockPhoto.com), 37d (Joe Gough – Fotolia.com), 37e (ninety99 – Fotolia.com), 37f (Alx – Fotolia.com), 37 bottom (P.Hussenot/photocuisine/Corbis), 41 (track5/iStockphoto.com), 42 (Hamish Blair/Getty Images Sport), 55t (Gina Martin/National Geographic Image Collection), 55c (Richard Olsenius/National Geographic Image Collection), 58tl (Jack Fletcher/National Geographic Image Collection), 58tr (Tino Soriano/National Geographic Image Collection), 58br (Randy Olson/National Geographic Image Collection), 59t (Joel Sartore/National Geographic Image Collection), 59b (Alaska Stock Images/National Geographic Image Collection), 65a (poco_bw – Fotolia.com), 65b (philsajonesen/iStockphoto.com), 65c (pamspix/iStockphoto.com), 66 (pamspix/iStockphoto.com), 66 1 (poco_bw – Fotolia.com), 66 2 (Alaska Stock Images/National Geographic Image Collection), 66 3 (pamspix/iStockphoto.com), 66 4 (pamspix/iStockphoto.com), 68 (Amine Boubnan – Fotolia.com), 69 (quix429/iStockphoto.com), 79 (megamix/iStockphoto.com), 90 (Magdalena Bujak. Image from BigStockPhoto.com), 97 Unit 1 (NASA/National Geographic Image Collection), 97 Unit 2 ([m] alex – Fotolia.com), 97 Unit 3 (KieselUndStein/iStockphoto.com), 97 Unit 4 (Phil Schermeister/National Geographic Image Collection), 97 Unit 5 (Ingo Arndt/Minden Pictures/National Geographic Image Collection), 97 Unit 6 (Ralph Lee Hopkins/National Geographic Image Collection), 97 Unit 7 (Patrick Bossert), 97 Unit 8 (courtesy of Terrafugia), 98a (Jason Edwards/National Geographic Image Collection), 98b (Michael Melford/National Geographic Image Collection), 98c (Medford Taylor/National Geographic Image Collection), 98d (Panoramic Stock Images/National Geographic Image Collection), 98 (NASA/National Geographic Image Collection), 98a (Gordon Wiltsie/National Geographic Image Collection), 99b (David Doubilet/National Geographic Image Collection), 99c (Richard Nowitz/National Geographic Image Collection), 99d (Frans Lanting/National Geographic Image Collection), 100a (Alaska Stock Images/National Geographic Image Collection), 100b ([m] alex – Fotolia.com), 101c (Beverly Joubert/National Geographic Image Collection), 101d (Carsten Peter/National Geographic Image Collection), 101 (joegough. Image from BigStockPhoto.com), 102a (Peter Menzel/Science Photo Library), 102b (Peter Menzel/Science Photo Library), 102c (Peter Menzel/Science Photo Library), 103d (Peter Menzel Photography), 103e (Michael Freeman/Corbis), 103f (Peter Menzel/Science Photo Library), 103 (KieselUndStein/iStockphoto.com), 104cr (Chris Schmick/Shutterstock, Inc), 104bl (Kevin Horan/National Geographic Image Collection), 104 (Kevin Horan/National Geographic Image Collection), 105a (Dauf – Fotolia.com), 105b (Emory Kristof/National Geographic Image Collection), 105c (eblue – Fotolia.com), 105d (Olga Besnard. Image from BigStockPhoto.com), 105e (Phil Schermeister/National Geographic Image Collection), 106 (Fabrice Beauchene – Fotolia.com), 106 (Ingo Arndt/Minden Pictures/National Geographic Image Collection), 106 (michealofiachra/iStockphoto.com), 106 (Tuy de Roy/Minden Pictures/National Geographic Image Collection), 107tr (Erlend Kvalsvik/iStockphoto.com), 107tl (Jeff Goldman/iStockphoto.com), 107bl (Jacynthroode/iStockphoto.com), 107br (Jacynthroode/iStockphoto.com), 107 (Jodi Cobb/National Geographic Image Collection), 108 (RTimages – Fotolia.com), 108a (George Steinmetz/National Geographic Image Collection), 108b (Ralph Lee Hopkins/National Geographic Image Collection), 108c (zxvisual/iStockphoto.com), 109d (Amon 1. Image from BigStockPhoto.com), 109e (Justin Guariglia/National Geographic Image Collection), 109f (han0747/iStockphoto.com), 109g (Annie Griffiths Belt/National Geographic Image Collection), 110a (Steve Winter Photography/National Geographic Image Collection), 110b (Patrick Bossert), 110c (Ian Howarth/National Geographic Image Collection), 111t (Patrick Bossert), 111l (Erik Freeland/National Geographic Image Collection), 111 (Rick Rickman/NewSport/Corbis), 112 3 (courtesy of Terrafugia), 112 4 (Daniel Dempster Photography/Alamy), 112 (AK2/iStockphoto.com)

Illustrations by Nigel Dobbyn pp 3, 10–11, 24, 32, 40 bottom, 87, 90, 91; Dylan Gibson pp 5, 7, 12, 30, 33, 43, 44, 47, 52, 53, 62, 63; Celia Hart pp 3, 18, 34, 46, 57, 86; Tim Kahane pp 40 (top), 84, 85, 88; Martin Sanders pp 8, 68; Eric Smith pp 22, 53, 54, 64, 66, 67, 74, 76, 77, 86; Simon Tegg p 52

Printed in the United Kingdom by Ashford Colour Press Ltd.
Print Number: 08   Print Year: 2023

My classroom

1 Find seven more classroom objects in the word square.

W	I	N	D	O	W	E
S	P	W	A	C	D	N
T	E	A	C	H	E	R
U	M	L	K	A	S	J
D	N	L	Q	I	K	D
E	O	S	U	R	T	U
N	B	O	A	R	D	S
T	I	V	R	L	W	E

2 Complete the words.

a b.ook............

1 a n.....................

2 a p.....................

3 a p.....................

4 a r.....................

5 a r.....................

6 a d.....................

7 a b.....................

The alphabet

3 ⊙**S1** Complete the alphabet. Then listen and check.

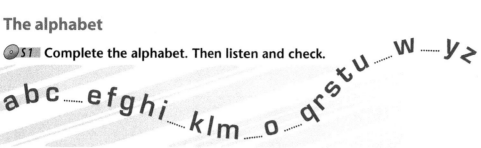

a b c ___ e f g h i ___ k l m ___ o ___ q r s t u ___ w ___ y z

4 Say the alphabet. Then complete the alphabet chart.

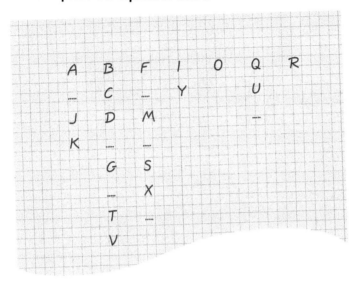

A	B	F	I	O	Q	R
___	C	___	Y		U	
J	D	M				___
K	___	___				
	G	S				
	___	X				
	T	___				
	V					

5 ⊙**S2** Listen and write the words.

1 .... *TV* ....   5 ....
2 ....   6 ....
3 ....   7 ....
4 ....   8 ....

6 Put the words and letters in the correct order.

A: How / spell / you / 'board'/ do?
A: ....
B: R-A-B-D-O
B: ....

Numbers

7 Look at the numbers. Write the words.

    1 .... *one* ....

a 3 ....   **j** 30 ....
b 5 ....   **k** 32 ....
c 8 ....   **l** 40 ....
d 11 ....   **m** 56 ....
e 12 ....   **n** 67 ....
f 13 ....   **o** 79 ....
g 15 ....   **p** 80 ....
h 20 ....   **q** 91 ....
i 24 ....   **r** 100 ....

8 Write the number of:

pages in this unit: .... *5-five* ....
a doors in your classroom: ....
b books in your bag: ....
c dictionaries in your classroom:
....
d pens on your desk: ....
e students in your class: ....
f people in your family: ....
g teachers in your school: ....
h letters in the alphabet: ....

Colours

9 Write the colours.

blue + red = ... *purple* ....
1 blue + yellow = ...
2 red + white = ...
3 red + ... = orange
4 .... + white = grey
5 red + green = ...

My school

Subject pronouns

1 Complete the table with these words.

| he | it | they | you | we |

Singular	Plural
I	....
you	....
....	
she	....
....	

2 Complete the sentences with subject pronouns.

Mr Brown's a teacher.

......*He*......'s a teacher.

1 The book's blue.

...................'s blue.

2 The walls in the classroom are green.

...................'re green.

3 Mrs Black is a teacher.

...................'s a teacher.

4 I am a student. David is a student.

...................'re students.

5 You speak English. Your teacher speaks English.

.... speak English.

6 The pencil's green.

...................'s green

Time

3 Write the times under the clocks.

It's quarter past eight.	It's ten to eleven.
It's half past two.	~~It's ten o'clock.~~
It's quarter to five.	It's twenty past nine.

4 Write the times in numbers.

It's half past six. ....*6.30*...........

1 It's quarter past eleven. ....

2 It's ten to one. ....

3 It's quarter past three. ....

4 It's twenty past five. ....

5 It's quarter to eight. ....

6 It's twenty to four. ....

7 It's eight o'clock. ....

8 It's five past five. ....

5 Write the times in words.

8.25 .....*twenty-five past eight*.....

1 7.30 ....

2 2.45 ....

3 1.15 ....

4 12.40 ....

5 11.50 ....

6 12.00 ....

7 8.05 ....

8 9.35 ....

6 ⊙**S3** Write the times you hear. Use numbers and words.

5.15 *Quarter past five*

1 ....

2 ....

3 ....

4 ....

5 ....

6 ....

7 ....

8 ....

.....*It's ten o'clock*.....

1 ....

2 ....

3 ....

4 ....

5 ....

Days and months

7 a **Find the days of the week in the word square.**

T	U	E	S	D	A	Y	W
T	H	C	A	W	M	A	W
S	O	S	L	E	O	V	E
U	A	A	M	R	N	N	D
N	I	T	B	U	D	B	N
D	L	F	U	K	A	J	E
A	A	D	C	R	Y	E	S
Y	O	R	A	V	D	I	D
F	R	I	D	A	Y	A	A
T	H	U	R	S	D	A	Y

b **Write the days in the correct order.**

1 ...... Monday ......   5 ....

2 ....   6 ....

3 ....   7 ....

4 ....

8 **Complete the months.**

1 J a n u a r y
2 F _ b r _ _ r y
3 M _ r c h
4 _ p r _ l
5 M _ y
6 J _ n _
7 J _ l y
8 _ _ g _ s t
9 S _ p t _ m b _ r
10 _ c t _ b _ r
11 N _ v _ m b _ r
12 D _ c _ m b _ r

9 **Look at the calendar for September. Circle the correct date.**

It's Friday, 2 /③/ 4 September.

1 It's Wednesday, 14 / 15 / 16 September.
2 It's Saturday, 25 / 26 / 27 September.
3 It's Thursday, 7 / 8 / 9 September.
4 It's Tuesday, 21 / 22 / 23 September.
5 It's Monday, 26 / 27 / 28 September.
6 It's Sunday, 5 / 6 / 7 September.

10 **Write the months.**

Christmas Day: 25 D.ecember ....

1 New Year: 1 J..................
2 Your birthday: ....

11 **Look at your diary and write the dates. Write the day, the date and the year.**

2/3 _Tuesday, 2 March 2010_ ....

1 28/7 ....
2 13/2 ....
3 24/6 ....
4 31/10 ....
5 13/5 ....
6 24/8 ....

12 **Complete the table.**
For days / months and verbs, write a word with the letter in it.
For colours and objects, write a word beginning with the letter.

	colour	day / month	verb	classroom / personal object
b		February		
r				ruler
p			speak	
w	white			

September

M		6	13	20	27
T		7	14	21	28
W	1	8	15	22	29
T	2	9	16	23	30
F	3	10	17	24	
S	4	11	18	25	
S	5	12	19	26	

Classroom language

1 **Match the expressions (1–5) with the pictures (a–e).**

1 Stand up. ......<i>c</i>......
2 Come here. ....
3 Write in your notebooks. ....
4 Sit down. ....
5 Don't talk. ....

2 **Complete the instructions. Match the verbs (1–6) with the expressions (a–f).**

1 Speak   **a** films in English.
2 Study   **b** your notebooks.
3 Don't write   **c** to the teacher.
4 Listen   **d** in the books.
5 Open   **e** at home.
6 Watch   **f** English in class.

3 **a** **Choose the correct words.**

Can I *borrow* / *watch* a pen?   *S*
1 Can you *mean* / *help* me?
2 I don't *understand* / *borrow*.
3 *Read* / *Help* in silence.
4 *Understand* / *Work* in pairs.
5 What does 'pairs' *speak* / *mean*, please?
6 *I'm* / *My* finished.
7 *Listen to* / *Open* me.
8 *Listen to* / *Look at* the board.

b **Now write *S* (Student) or *T* (Teacher) next to the sentences.**

4 **Write the negative forms.**

Open the book.
...........<i>Don't</i>........... open the book.
1 Write in the book.
.... in the book.
2 Look at the board.
.... at the board.
3 Listen to Maria.
.... to Maria.

1A Welcome!

Vocabulary: adjectives

1 Find nine more adjectives in the word chain. Write the words.

tiredsadtallhungryhappyshortfairdarkthinold

......*tired*......   **5** ....

1 ....   **6** ....

2 ....   **7** ....

3 ....   **8** ....

4 ....   **9** ....

Vocabulary: countries

2 Circle the country where English isn't the language.

England	Australia	New Zealand	Ireland
Austria	Canada	Scotland	

3 a Match the languages (1–9) with the countries (a–i).

1 French   **a** the Czech Republic

2 Polish   **b** Germany

3 German   **c** Greece

4 Portuguese   **d** Holland

5 Greek   **e** Hungary

6 Dutch   **f** Poland

7 Spanish   **g** Portugal

8 Czech   **h** France

9 Hungarian   **i** Spain

b Now find the countries on the map.

Study tip!

In English, languages always start with a capital letter.

Vocabulary: family relationships

4 Find nine more family words in the word square. Write the words.

A	U	T	U	D	A	D	U	T	H	R	E
G	R	A	N	D	P	A	R	E	N	T	S
N	I	E	C	E	S	U	M	O	I	F	O
T	D	F	L	C	F	G	H	N	S	A	N
U	S	T	E	M	A	H	F	A	U	H	N
A	U	C	L	N	T	T	C	U	O	E	E
S	I	N	E	P	H	E	W	G	C	W	P
F	M	O	T	H	E	R	H	D	U	S	M
A	U	N	T	W	R	L	G	P	F	A	H

......*dad*......   ....

....

....

....

....

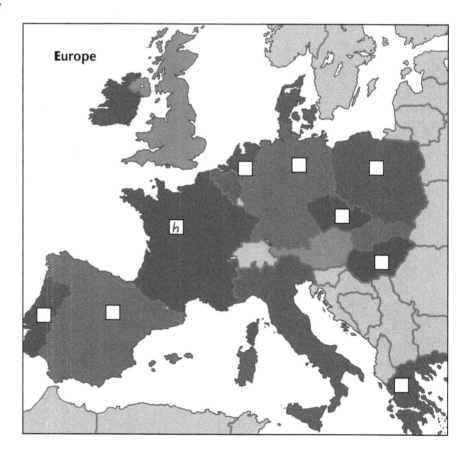

Europe

Grammar: *be* (affirmative)

5 Complete the table with short forms.

Long form	Short form
I am	I'm
you are	you...
he/she/it is	he/she/it...
we are	we...
you are	you...
they are	they...

Grammar: *be* (negative)

6 Write the negative forms of *be* in the table.

	Long form	Short form
I	I am not	I'm not
you	you are not	
he/she/it		
we		
you		
they		

Grammar: *be* (short forms)

7 Complete the profile with affirmative short forms.

I'm Carlo. I ...*'m*... thirteen. I [1] .... from Australia. My mother [2] .... from Sydney. My father [3] .... from Italy. Maria and Roberto are my cousins. They [4] .... from Italy too. We [5] .... at my cousin's house in Palermo. It [6] .... a small house. We [7] .... very happy.

8 Complete the sentences with negative short forms.

Carlo ....*isn't*.......... from Italy.

1 Carlo's mother .... from Palermo.
2 Carlo's father .... from Sydney.
3 Maria and Roberto .... from Australia.

Grammar: *be* (questions and short answers)

9 Put the words in order to make questions.

from / Carlo / Australia? / is
Is Carlo from Australia?

1 twelve? / is / Carlo

....

2 Maria and Roberto / are / Australian?

....

3 big? / is / the house

....

4 are / sad? / they

....

10 Now write short answers to the questions in Exercise 9.

Is Carlo from Australia? *Yes, he is.*

1 ....
2 ....
3 ....
4 ....

1B This is my family

Reading and listening

1 **🔵1.1** Read and listen to the dialogue. Find the people in the photo.

Ryan: This is a photo of my family. These are my grandparents. They're from Holland. My grandfather's really old. He's 83. That's my mum. She's their daughter. She's tall and fair.

Alice: Is your dad tall?

Ryan: No, he isn't. He's short and dark. And that's my aunt Kate. She's short and dark too.

Alice: Who's that?

Ryan: That's my brother, Scott. He's tall and fair. And that's my sister, Megan. We're dark and thin. Megan isn't happy.

Alice: Is that your cousin?

Ryan: No, it isn't. That's my niece, Rosie. She's one. I'm her uncle! Scott is her dad. Her mum, Jane, is a doctor.

2 Look at the photo and read the dialogue again. Label the people. Use these words. There are two extra words!

sister	brother	~~grandfather~~
dad	uncle	niece	mum
aunt	cousin	

3 Read the dialogue again. Are the sentences true or false?

	T	F
Megan is happy.	☐	☑
1 Megan and Ryan are dark and thin.	☐	☐
2 Megan and Ryan's grandparents are from Holland.	☐	☐
3 Scott is Ryan's uncle.	☐	☐
4 Rosie isn't Ryan's cousin.	☐	☐

Ryan's family

Scott – ....
Gloria – ....
Me – Ryan
Megan – ....
Jack – grandfather
Kate – ....
Robert – ....
Rosie – ....

Listening

4 a 🔘 **1.2** **Listen to the dialogue. Are the sentences true or false?**

	T	F
Ryan's cousins are from Holland.	✔	☐
1 Karin is short and dark.	☐	☐
2 Petra is tall and dark.	☐	☐
3 It's Petra's birthday.	☐	☐

b Listen again and correct the false sentences.

....

....

Grammar: possessive adjectives

5 Complete the table with these words.

~~my~~	our	your	her
your	their	his	its

Subject Pronouns	Possessive Adjectives
I	.........my.........
you	....
he	....
she	....
it	....
we	....
you	....
they	....

6 Complete the profile with these words.

his	your	~~my~~	their	their
our	our	her		

..........My.......... name's Sarah. I'm sixteen. My brother's twenty-two. ¹.......................... name's Ewan. My sister's fifteen. ².......................... name's Nicola. We're from England. ³.......................... cousins are from Canada. ⁴.......................... dad is English. He's ⁵.......................... uncle. ⁶.......................... mum isn't English. She's Canadian. Where are you from? Where is ⁷.......................... family from?

Grammar: *this, that, these, those*

7 Complete the sentences with *this, that, these* or *those*.

......*Those*...... are my suitcases.

1 .... is my cat.

2 .... are my friends.

3 .... elephant is enormous.

4 What's .... ?

Susan – grandmother

Jane

1 Complete the identity card with these words.

| ~~first name~~ | postcode | surname |
| date of birth | country | address |

first name   Mairi
1   Toibin
2   30/10/1990
3   Ireland
4   21 Green Street Dublin
5   D16

2 Match the questions (1–7) with the answers (a–h). There is one extra answer!

1 What's your name?
2 What's your surname?
3 How do you spell that?
4 Where are you from?
5 What's your address?
6 What's your telephone number?
7 How old are you?

a Twenty-three.
b 896743324.
c B-R-double O-K-E-S.
d Brookes.
e 16/06/1985.
f Hal.
g 44 School Lane, Toronto.
h Canada.

3 Choose the best response for each statement.

Hello, Max! Welcome to Wellington!
(a) Hello, Jim! Thanks.
b Welcome to Wellington.
c Let's go.

1 I'm from London. And you?
  a Nice to meet you.
  b Are you OK?
  c I'm from Los Angeles.
2 Hi, Sandra. This is my friend, Daisy.
  a I'm tired!
  b Nice to meet you!
  c Thanks, Daisy.
3 Daisy's from Canada.
  a Good afternoon.
  b My mum's over there.
  c Where are you from in Canada, Daisy?

4 1.3 Listen. Choose the correct picture.

5 🔘 **1.3 Listen again. Are the sentences true or false?**

	T	F
Will is from England.	☐	☑
1 Amy is Sally's sister.	☐	☐
2 Will's suitcases are small.	☐	☐
3 Sally's dad is at the airport.	☐	☐

Pronunciation: *is* and *are*

6 🔘 **1.4 Listen. Practise saying the sentences.**

1 Jill is in India.

2 Istanbul isn't in Italy.

3 My father is dark.

4 Martha and Mark are in the park.

Writing: punctuation

7 **Rewrite the sentences with capital letters.**

i'm from italy. *I'm from Italy.*

1 my best friends are eric and meera.

....

2 my address is 16 east street.

....

3 my father is from manchester.

....

4 basketball is on friday.

....

5 it's cold in december.

....

Writing: personal information

8 **Complete the table. Write about yourself.**

your name	your age	your appearance	where you are from
Andrew	thirteen	short, fair	Bristol, England

9 **Complete the table. Write about your family and friends.**

their names	their ages	their appearance	where they are from
my mum	forty-seven	short, red-haired	London
1			
2			
3			
4			

10 **Write sentences about your family. Use the information from Exercises 8 and 9.**

My name is Andrew. I'm 13. I'm short and fair. I'm from Bristol in England.

My mum is 47. She's short and red-haired. She's from London.

....

....

....

....

....

....

....

....

....

....

....

....

....

....

....

....

Listening

1 🔘 **1.5 a Listen to Colleen. What is she talking about?**

   a her family

   b her appearance

   c her city

b Match these words with the headings and complete the table.

| buildings | beautiful | parents | sister | capital |
| tall | parks | thin | big | brother | cousins | river |

family	cities	adjectives
....	*buildings*	....
....	....	....
....	....	....
....	....	....

 Tip! You can use the adjective *beautiful* to talk about people <u>and</u> cities.

2 🔘 **1.5 Look at the words below. Listen to Colleen again. Circle the words you hear.**

buildings

beautiful   parents

sister   capital   tall   parks

thin   big   brother

cousins   river

3 **Now do this exercise.**

🔘 **1.6 Listen to Sathya. What is she talking about?**

   a her appearance

   b her city

   c her family

4 **Now do this exercise.**

🔘 **1.7 Listen to Alex. Where is he?**

   a in the USA

   b in Australia

   c in England

5 Read this email from Alex. Choose the correct words.

1 Alex is in *Australia / New Zealand*.

2 He's on the *North / South* Island.

3 His parents are in *New Zealand / England*.

```
⊝ ⊝ ⊝                                                     ⊝

To: keithbrenda@mail.com
From: xela1@mail.com
Subject: Hello again.

Hi Mum and Dad,

How are you? How's England? I'm not in Australia at the moment. I'm in
Wellington with my friend, Jenny. It's the capital city of New Zealand. It
isn't a very big city. It's on the North Island and it's near the sea. New
Zealand is really beautiful and green.

Love,

Alex
```

6 Read the email again and choose the correct answer (a, b or c).

What is Alex writing about?

a Jenny

b New Zealand

c England

7 Now do these exercises.

1 Read the text. Who is Annie?

   a a scientist

   b a chimpanzee

   c a famous person

2 Read the text again. Who are Keira and Angelina?

   a Annie's daughters

   b Meryl's daughters

   c Brad and Tom's cousins

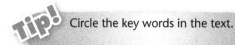 Circle the key words in the text.

My name's Annie Twigg and I'm a scientist. The chimpanzees in the photo are from Africa. They're a family. They're brothers and sisters. Their names are Tom, Brad, Keira and Angelina. They're happy. Their mother is in the photo too. Her name's Meryl.

Grammar Practice | Unit 1

be (affirmative)

The present simple of *be* has three forms: *am*, *are* and *is*.

I am a boy/girl.
You/We/They are French.
He/She/It is tall.

> In English, we use *you* for one person (singular) or for lots of people (plural). The verb form for *you* singular and *you* plural is always the same.

We use *be* to talk about names, ages, nationalities, jobs, etc. We also use *be* to describe people and things.

I am Gareth.   *I am thirteen.*
I am from Wales.   *I am tall and dark-haired.*

We use the **short form** in everyday language.

Hi – I'm Harry.   *You're funny!*
He's at school.   *We're fourteen.*

Long form	Short form
I am	I'm
you are	you're
he is	he's
she is	she's
it is	it's
we are	we're
you are	you're
they are	they're

Affirmative		
I'm (I am)	We're (We are)	
You're (You are)	You're (You are)	
He's (He is) She's (She is) It's (It is)	They're (They are)	from New Zealand.

1 Choose the correct words.

His name is Michel. It am / are / <u>is</u> a French name.
1 You **am** / **are** / **is** a good basketball player.
2 This is Francesca. She **am** / **are** / **is** my aunt.
3 Mum, we **am** / **are** / **is** hungry!
4 Is that your brother? He **am** / **are** / **is** very tall!
5 I **am** / **are** / **is** from Scotland.
6 Those are my friends. They **am** / **are** / **is** in my class.

2 Now complete the sentences with short forms.

His name is Michel. It ..'s.. a French name.
1 You ...... a good basketball player.
2 This is Francesca. She ...... my aunt.
3 Mum, we ...... hungry!
4 Is that your brother? He ...... very tall!
5 I ...... from Scotland.
6 Those are my friends. They ..... in my class.

be (negative)

We make the negative of *be* by adding the word *not* after *am/are/is*.

> Notice the short form of *are* and *is* in the negative:
>
> *I'm not hungry.*   *You/We/They aren't tired.*
> *He/She/It isn't old.*

Negative		
I'm not	(am not)	a basketball player.
You/We/They aren't	(are not)	very happy.
He/She/It isn't	(is not)	from France.

3 Complete the sentences with negative short forms.

Carl ...*isn't*... my cousin – he's my friend.
1 My parents .... teachers – they're doctors.
2 It .... your book – it's my book!
3 Jane .... from Canada – she's Australian.
4 I .... English – I'm from the USA.
5 We .... fair-haired – we're dark-haired.
6 You .... sixteen – you're only twelve!
7 I .... sad – I'm very happy.
8 New Delhi .... in the USA – it's in India.

be (questions and short answers)

We make questions by putting *am/are/is* before the subject (*I, you/we/they, he/she/it*).

Affirmative: *They are my friends.*
Question: *Are they my friends?*

> We don't use short forms (*I'm, you're*, etc) with affirmative short answers.

Questions	
Am I	
Are you/we/they	from America?
Is he/she/it	
Short answers	
Yes, I am.	No, I'm not.
Yes, he/she/it is.	No, he/she/it isn't.
Yes, you/we/they are.	No, you/we/they aren't.

4 **Write questions from these sentences.**

Clark is a scientist. *Is Clark a scientist?*

1 She's a basketball player.

....

2 It's your cat.

....

3 I'm a member of the library.

....

4 You're their cousin.

....

5 They're brother and sister.

....

5 **Put the words in the correct order to make questions.**

Los Angeles / in / is / the USA?

Is Los Angeles in the USA?

1 we / friends / are?

....

2 I / am / tired?

....

3 Martha and Clark / Antarctica / are / in?

....

4 Maria / is / French?

....

5 is / fair-haired / your brother?

....

6 **Now write affirmative (✔) or negative (✗) short answers to the questions in Exercise 5.**

(Is Los Angeles in the USA?) (✔) *Yes, it is.*

1 (✔) ....

2 (✗) ....

3 (✔) ....

4 (✗) ....

5 (✔) ....

7 **Write questions (?), affirmative (✔) and negative (✗) sentences with these words. Use short forms.**

he / your cousin (?) *Is he your cousin?*

Anna / from Hull (✗) *Anna isn't from Hull.*

1 my aunt / a teacher (✔)

....

2 I / from India (✗)

....

3 we / basketball players (✗)

....

4 they / in the Antarctic (✔)

....

5 your suitcase / blue (?)

....

Possessive adjectives

We use a **possessive adjective** before a noun to say who/what it belongs to or is related to.

I'm from Spain. **My** <u>home</u> *is in Madrid.*

He's red-haired. **His** <u>hair</u> *is red.*

We're students. **Our** <u>teacher</u> *is Miss Stanton.*

They're my friends. **Their** <u>names</u> *are Becky and Tom.*

Subject pronouns							
I	you	he	she	it	we	you	they
Possessive adjectives							
my	your	his	her	its	our	your	their

8 **Complete the sentences with possessive adjectives.**

My surname is Jenkins. What's .....*your*.... surname?

1 He's my cousin. .... mother is my aunt.

2 We're English. .... home is in London.

3 Hi! I'm from Spain and .... name is Miguel.

4 This is my sister Pilar. .... hair is very short!

5 They're my friends and this is .... house.

9 **Complete the dialogue with *its*, *it's*, *your* and *you're*.**

Sandra: Hi – I'm Sandra. What's .....*your*.... name?

Kezia: Hello. I'm Kezia.

Sandra: Oh, (1) .... the new student! Well, here's (2) .... classroom.

Kezia: (3) .... a beautiful school.

Sandra: Yes, it is. (4) .... buildings are very old.

this, that, these, those

We use **this** to talk about one person/thing near us, and **that** to talk about one person/thing far away.

We use **these** to talk about more than one person/thing near us, and **those** to talk about more than one person/thing far away.

10 **Complete the sentences with *this, that, these* or *those*.**

What's .....*this*..... thing here?

1 Who is .... girl in the library?

2 Hi, Mum! .... are my friends, Katie and Sue.

3 Here – .... is a photo of my family.

4 Look! Is .... your suitcase?

5 .... are my parents, over there.

2A Let's go

Vocabulary: possessions

1 Label the pictures.

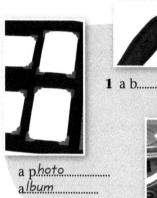

a p*hoto*............
a *lbum*............

1 a b............

2 a c............

3 a m............
p............

4 a r............

5 a t............

6 a w............

7 a c............

2 Write the names of the possessions in the table.

b

Bag a	Bag b
MP3	....
....	....
....	....
....	....
....	....

a

3 Complete the dialogue with these words.

| sure | borrow | let's | ~~ready~~ |
| credit | late | wait | |

A: The taxi's here. Are you ......*ready*...... ?

B: Yes.

A: OK. ¹............ go!

B: ²............ a moment! I haven't got ³............ on my mobile.

A: That's OK. You can ⁴............ my phone.

B: Thanks.

A: Are you ⁵............ you've got everything now?

B: Yes! Come on. We're ⁶............ !

Grammar: *have got* (affirmative and negative)

4 **Write the short forms.**

I have got a brother and a sister.
..........*I've got*.......... a brother and a sister.

1 We have not got a car.
.... a car.

2 He has got a computer.
.... a computer.

3 It has got games on it.
.... games on it.

4 My sister has not got a motorbike.
My sister .... a motorbike.

5 My parents have not got a motorbike.
My parents .... a motorbike.

6 They have got a car.
.... a car.

7 We have got a cat.
.... a cat.

5 **Complete the text. Use short forms.**

> Hello. I'm Ella
> and this is my sister, Sandra.
> We'....*ve got*....... a big bedroom. It
> ¹........................... two beds and one desk with
> two chairs. We ²........................... a computer and a
> CD player, but we ³........................... a TV. Sandra
> ⁴........................... a camera and a photo album. She
> ⁵........................... a poster of Brad Pitt on the wall. I
> ⁶........................... a photo of my friends. They're
> in Italy and they ⁷........................... big
> ice creams!

Grammar: *have got* (questions and short answers)

6 **Write questions with these words.**

Sandra and Ella / a TV?
................*Have Sandra and Ella got a TV?*................

1 you / an MP3?
....

2 Sandra / a poster of Brad Pitt?
....

3 Ella and Sandra / a computer?
....

4 your dad / a motorbike?
....

5 you and your family / a car?
....

7 **Now write short answers to the questions in Exercise 6.**

..........*No, they haven't.*.....

1 ....

2 ....

3 ....

4 ....

5 ....

8 **What is the full form of *'s*? Tick the correct box.**

	is	has
Sandra's thirteen.	✔	☐
1 She's got a camera.	☐	☐
2 Her sister's fifteen.	☐	☐
3 She's got a computer.	☐	☐
4 Their bedroom's big.	☐	☐
5 It's got two beds.	☐	☐

Reading and listening

1 ⊙ **2.1** Read and listen to Amy, Ben and Marcus. Choose the best heading. There is one extra heading.

My photos	My family
~~My toys~~	My music

1 My toys
I've got a collection of old toys. I've got toys from all over the world. Some of them are very old. This toy car is from Germany. It's really old and valuable. Look! This is my favourite toy. It's a toy elephant from India.

Amy

2 ....
I've got about 300 CDs and records in my collection. My favourite CD is by James Brown. It's really great. Some of the records are from my grandfather. I've also got records by Elvis, Buddy Holly and Frank Sinatra. They're really old and some of them are valuable.

Ben

3 ....
I've got about 20 photo albums and about 400 photos. Look! This is a photo of my grandparents in France. My grandfather's from Holland. His brother and his wife have got a farm in the south of Holland. And these are photos of our family holiday in Paris. Can you see the Eiffel Tower?

Marcus

2 Read the texts. Who are the sentences about? Write their names.

Who has got a valuable toy car?	Amy
1 Who has got a collection of records?	....
2 Who has got a photo of Paris?	....
3 Who has got about 400 photos?	....
4 Who has got an elephant from India?	....
5 Who has got a CD by James Brown?	....

Grammar: indefinite articles *a* and *an*

3 Complete the text. Write *a*, *an* or – (no article).

I've got ......a...... mobile phone. It's really cool. It's got ¹............. MP3 player and I've got ²............. songs by Coldplay on it. It's got ³............. camera but it hasn't got ⁴............. video camera. It's also got ⁵............. computer, with email. Look! I've got ⁶............. messages! They're from ⁷............. friend in Brazil.

Grammar: *can*

4 Match the verbs (1–10) with the words (a–j).

1	cook	**a**	a car
2	copy	**b**	a computer
3	send	**c**	the piano
4	make	**d**	Spanish
5	play	**e**	an email
6	use	**f**	a pizza
7	drive	**g**	a CD
8	speak	**h**	clothes
9	climb	**i**	cakes
10	wash	**j**	trees

5 Make true sentences. Circle *can* or *can't*.

I *can* / *can't* cook a pizza.

1 My mum *can* / *can't* copy a CD.

2 My dad *can* / *can't* play the piano.

3 My cousin *can* / *can't* climb trees.

4 My grandmother *can* / *can't* speak Spanish.

6 Write about two people in your family. Write two sentences about each person.

My sister can cook a pizza. She can't drive a car.

1 ....

....

2 ....

....

7 Write questions with these words. Then write short answers.

your mum / make cakes?
Can your mum make cakes?
Yes, she can.

1 you / use a computer?

....

....

2 your grandmother / climb a mountain?

....

....

3 cats / play the piano?

....

....

4 you and your friends / play basketball?

....

....

Can you dance?
Can you sing?
Can you act?
Be on top TV show
Britain's Got Talent.
Click here for details.

Amanda can act and she can dance. She's on the TV programme, *Britain's Got Talent*.

She can sing too. She's really got talent! Can she win the first prize on the TV show? No, she can't — she's a judge!

8 Write affirmative sentences (✔) and questions (?) with these words.

Amanda / sing. *Amanda can sing.*

1 Amanda / act? ....

2 Amanda / dance? ....

3 we / dance / salsa ....

4 you / sing / opera? ....

5 they / act ....

9 Can you win *Britain's Got Talent*? Write two sentences with *can* and two sentences with *can't*.

I can sing. I can't sing opera.

....

....

....

....

1 Write requests with *can* and these words.

Mum, / you / drive / me / to school?

Mum, can you drive me to school?

1 I / borrow / a pen?

....

2 I / use / your dictionary?

....

3 I / have / some pizza, please?

....

4 I / borrow / your umbrella?

....

2 Complete the dialogues with these words.

course	excuse	I	sorry
~~can~~	help	credit	where

A: It's very hot. ..*Can*.... you open the window?

B: Yes, of ^{1}.............. .

A: I haven't got ^{2}.............. on my mobile. Can I use your phone?

B: No! I'm ^{3}.............. , you can't.

A: Mum, I can't find my bag. Can you ^{4}.............. me?

B: No, I'm sorry! ^{5}.............. can't.

A: ^{6}.............. me. I'm lost. Can you help me?

B: Of course. ^{7}.............. do you want to go?

Pronunciation: *can* and *can't*

3 🔘 **2.2** Listen and repeat.

1 Can you help me?

2 Yes, I can.

3 Sorry, I can't.

4 I can't speak Spanish.

5 Can you dance?

6 No, I can't.

7 I can play the guitar. Can you?

8 No, I can't. But I can play the piano.

Vocabulary: months

4 Find the months in the word chain and write them in the correct order.

marchjunefebruaryaugustdecemberseptemberaprilijulyoctobermayjanuarynovember

1 .... *January* ....
2 ....
3 ....
4 ....
5 ....
6 ....

7 ....
8 ....
9 ....
10 ....
11 ....
12 ....

Vocabulary: ordinal numbers

5 Look at the example. Write the dates in full.

1/11   *The first of November*

1 3/3 ....
2 15/5 ....
3 12/8 ....
4 20/10 ....
5 21/2 ....

6 Complete the dialogue. Use the responses in the box.

D-E-B-O-R-A-H.
~~Yes, of course.~~
It's on the ninth of May.
It's Deborah.

A: Excuse me. Can I ask you some questions?
B: ...*Yes, of course*...
A: What's your name?
B: [1]...
A: Can you spell that, please?
B: [2]...
A: When's your birthday?
B: [3]...

Writing: a thank-you letter

7 Complete the thank-you letter with these words.

six	great	seventh	favourite

Dear Aunt Mabel,
Thank you for the Harry Potter
book. Harry Potter's my [1].....................
hero.
I've got the first [2]..................... books.
This is the [3]..................... book. It's
[4].....................!
Thanks again.
Love,
Billy

Listening

1 Look at the picture of Jenny and her mum. Jenny is going shopping with a friend at eleven o'clock. She's ready to go. What has Jenny got?

1 A bag ☐
2 A camera ☐
3 A phone ☐
4 An umbrella ☐

2 **2.3** Listen to Jenny and her mum. What has Jenny got? Choose the correct answer.

a Jenny's got a bag and a camera.

b Jenny's got a bag and an umbrella.

c Jenny's got a phone and a camera.

3 Now do these exercises.

1 **2.4** Listen to Ben and James. What can James borrow? Circle the correct answer.

a James can borrow a Coldplay CD.

b James can borrow a Metallica CD.

c James can borrow a CD by Duffy.

2 **2.5** Listen to Harry and Maria. What can Harry's grandmother do? Circle the correct answer.

a She can play the piano.

b She can make chocolate cakes.

c She can play basketball.

3 **2.6** Listen to Julia and Helen. What can't Julia do? Circle the correct answer.

a She can't dance and she can't sing.

b She can't sing and she can't act.

c She can't play the guitar and she can't dance.

Tip! Remember to read the three answers before you listen.

4 **Complete the postcard from Kerry. Choose the correct option.**

Hi Mum and Dad,

We're in Australia. It's fantastic!
The animals ¹*are / is* amazing.
This postcard ²*has / have* got a
picture of ³*kangaroo / kangaroos*
on it. They ⁴*can / can't* jump
across long distances.

See you soon,

Love,

Kerry

Mr and Mrs Prince

21 Parrot Road

Liverpool,

England

Greetings from Australia

5 **Now do these exercises.**

1 Complete the text by filling in each gap (1–3) with the correct form of these words.

have   be   can

My favourite animals ¹............................ kangaroos.
They ²............................ got enormous feet. They
can jump but they ³............................ run.

2 Complete the text by filling in each gap (1–3) with the correct form of these words.

can   be   building

Storks ¹............................ big birds. They
²............................ fly. You can see them at the top
of tall ³............................ .

3 Complete the text by filling in each gap (1–3) with the correct form of these words.

be   have   library

My city ¹............................ got two ²............................ .
They ³............................ big. You can borrow books
and CDs.

Grammar Practice Unit 2

have got (affirmative and negative)

The present simple of **have got** has two forms: **have got** and **has got**.

I/You/We/They **have got** *a piano.*
He/She/It **has got** *long legs.*

We use **have got** to talk about someone's things or to describe someone or something.

I've got a new watch.
Harry has got dark hair.

We use the short form in everyday language.

Long form	Short form
I have	I've
you have	you've
he has	he's
she has	she's
it has	it's
we have	we've
they have	they've

> Be careful with **it's** *(it has)* **got** and **it's** *(it has)*.

The negative is **haven't** *(have not)* **got** or **hasn't** *(has not)* **got**.

Affirmative	
I've/You've/We've/They've got (I/You/We/They have got)	a camera.
He's/She's/It's got (He/She/It has got)	an Italian name.
Negative	
I/You/We/They haven't got (have not got) He/She/It hasn't got (has not got)	a key.

1 Complete the sentences with *have* or *has*.

Anna ....*has*............ got her travel card.
1 We .... not got an MP3.
2 I .... got an umbrella in my suitcase.
3 They .... got a new computer.
4 Your mobile .... not got a camera.
5 He .... got a collection of toy cars.
6 You .... got a beautiful house.

2 Write affirmative (✔) or negative (✘) sentences with these words. Use short forms.

I / an American cousin ✔
............*I've got an American cousin.*............
1 they / a house in France. ✔
....
2 I / credit on my mobile. ✘
....
3 Jane / a big bedroom. ✔
....
4 you / my mobile! ✔
....
5 he / his key. ✘
....

have got (questions and short answers)

We make questions by putting **have/has** before the subject, and then **got**.

We don't use short forms (*I've, you've,* etc) with affirmative short answers.

Questions			
Have Has	I/you/we/they he/she/it	got	any food?
Short answers			
Yes, I/you/we/they have. Yes, he/she/it has.		No, I/you/we/they haven't. No, he/she/it hasn't.	

3 Write questions from these sentences.

You've got an umbrella.
Have you got an umbrella?
1 She's got posters on her bedroom wall.
....
2 We've got an English lesson on Monday.
....
3 He's got a library card.
....
4 That cat's got blue eyes!
....
5 They've got lots of games on their computer.
....

4 Write questions with these words.

your mum / an MP3?

Has your mum got an MP3?

1 Brad / red hair?

....

2 we / a cake?

....

3 your grandparents / a dog?

....

4 you / an unusual pet?

....

5 she / a photo album?

....

5 Now write affirmative (✔) or negative (✗) short answers to the questions in Exercise 4.

(Has your mum got an MP3?) ✗ ...*No, she hasn't.*...

1 ✔ ....

2 ✗ ....

3 ✔ ....

4 ✗ ....

5 ✔ ....

indefinite articles *a* and *an*

We use *a* with singular nouns that start with a **consonant** sound (*b, c, d, f, g, etc*).

a book   *a cat*   *a dog*   *a friend*   *a girl etc*

We use *an* with singular nouns that start with a **vowel** sound (*a, e, i, o, u*).

an apple   *an email*   *an ice cream*
an orange   *an umbrella*

We don't use *a* or *an* with plural nouns (apples, books, cats, etc).

6 Complete the sentences with *a, an* or – (no article).

I've got ....*a*.............. mobile in my pocket.

1 She's got .... uncle in the USA.

2 Some people have got .... snakes as pets!

3 They've got .... piano.

4 You haven't got .... posters in your bedroom.

5 Harry's got .... collection of toy cars.

6 I've got .... umbrella in my suitcase.

can

Can has the same form for all subjects (*I, you, he, etc*). The main verb after *can* is in the **bare infinitive**.

I/We/She/etc can make/do/go/etc ...

We use *can* to talk or ask about ability.

*She **can** sing very well.*   *__Can__ you speak Italian?*

We also use *can* to make and answer requests.

*__Can__ I use your pencil, please? – Yes, you **can**.*
*__Can__ you help me, please? – Yes, of course I **can** help you.*

The negative of *can* is *can't (cannot)* and it is the same for all subjects.

Affirmative		Negative	
I/You/We/They He/She/It	can swim.	I/You/We/They He/She/It	can't (cannot) swim.

We make questions by putting *can* before the subject, and then the bare infinitive of the main verb.

Questions		
Can	I/you/we/they he/she/it	swim?
Short answers		

Yes,	I/you/we/they	can.	No,	I/you/we/they he/she/it	can't.

7 Write sentences with these words. Use *can* (✔) or *can't* (✗).

I / send an email ✔

......*I can send an email.*......

1 my parents / drive a car. ✔

....

2 some birds / fly. ✗

....

3 some parrots / speak. ✔

....

4 we / use a microwave. ✔

....

5 he / play the piano. ✗

....

8 Write questions with these words.

Brad / play basketball?

Can Brad play basketball?

1 your friends / sing?

....

2 Harry / ride a motorbike?

....

3 her mum / make a cake?

....

4 we / speak Italian?

....

5 your dog / swim?

....

Review Units 1 and 2

1 Complete the sentences with the correct form of *be*.

1 I .... very tired.
2 Mr Kelly .... from England
3 We .... not brother and sister.
4 My grandparents .... very old.
5 My cousin .... twelve years old.

1 mark per item: ... / 5 marks

2 Choose the correct words.

1 Danny is short. **His/He** father is very tall.
2 We are American. **We/Our** parents are from Los Angeles.
3 Hi, I'm Billy. What's **you/your** name?
4 Mr Brown is **me/my** teacher.
5 Lisa and Mona are sisters. **They're/Their** both very short.

1 mark per item: ... / 5 marks

3 Choose the correct words.

1 Where's **this/those** boy from? Is he from Australia?
2 Look at **that/those** girls! They're very thin.
3 Hi, Steve. **This/Those** is my uncle Tom.
4 What's **this/those** girl's name?
5 Hello, Ms Parker! **This/These** are my friends from school.

1 mark per item: ... / 5 marks

4 Complete the questions and short answers.

1 .... Jenny from the USA?
Yes, ...
2 .... Dave and Carol in London?
No, ...
3 .... Simon your best friend?
Yes, ...
4 .... your sister tall and red-haired?
No, ...
5 .... Carlos and his sisters from Brazil?
Yes, ...

2 marks per item: ... / 10 marks

5 Write questions using the correct form of *have got* with these words.

1 your cousins / a computer?
....
2 your friend / a cat?
....
3 you / a pen?
....
4 your sister / a camera?
....
5 your mum and dad / jobs?
....

1 mark per item: ... / 5 marks

6 Complete the sentences with *a, an* or – (no article).

1 I've got .... mobile phone in my handbag.
2 Carol hasn't got .... dress for the party.
3 They've got .... old computer.
4 Dave's got .... email from his cousin.
5 She's got .... toy from her childhood.

1 mark per item: ... / 5 marks

7 Write sentences or questions with *can*.

1 I/draw/pictures.
....
2 you/help me, please?
....
3 My brother and sister/speak German.
....
4 your cousin/drive?
....
5 Paul/not/swim.
....

1 mark per item: ... / 5 marks

8 Complete the sentences with *can, can't, are* or *aren't*.

1 .... their cousins from Spain?
2 I .... drive a car or swim.
3 We .... speak English and Italian.
4 They .... from Australia. They're from Canada.
5 He hasn't got a computer. He .... use the Internet.

2 marks per item: ... / 10 marks

9 Complete the sentences.

1 Amy is not short. She is ....
2 Gary is .... He isn't fat.
3 Jack is .... , not fair.
4 Tina and Anna are not sad. They are ....
5 The house isn't small. It is ....

1 mark per item: ... / 5 marks

10 Match the words.

1 grandfather ...   **a** sister
2 mother ...   **b** nephew
3 brother ...   **c** grandmother
4 niece ...   **d** daughter
5 son ...   **e** father

1 mark per item: ... / 5 marks

11 Complete the sentences with these countries.

| Australia   Brazil   England |
| New Zealand   the USA |

1 Peter is from New York in ....
2 London is the capital of ....
3 Mary's father is from Rio de Janeiro in ....
4 My favourite city is Wellington in ....
5 My friend Brad is from Sydney in ....

1 mark per item: ... / 5 marks

12 Complete the sentences using five of these words.

| doctor   fair   father |
| parents   son   surname |

1 What's her .... ?
2 Laura's aunt is a ....
3 My .... are from India.
4 Amanda is short and ....
5 Harry is the eleven-year-old .... of Mrs Bradley.

2 marks per item: ... / 10 marks

13 Complete the sentences using these words.

| bag   keys   mobile   purse   watch |

1 I keep my money in a ....
2 My books are in my ....
3 Have you got .... to the house?
4 What's the time? Have you got a .... on?
5 I haven't got credit on my .... phone.

1 mark per item: ... / 5 marks

14 Complete the sentences using these words.

| drive   fly   send   swim   use |

1 Superman can .... through the sky.
2 My brother can .... in the sea.
3 My grandmother can't .... emails.
4 My dad can .... a car.
5 Paula can't .... a microwave.

1 mark per item: ... / 5 marks

15 Write the ordinal numbers.

1 one   ....
2 three   ....
3 thirteen   ....
4 twenty   ....
5 thirty-one   ....

1 mark per item: ... / 5 marks

16 Write the sentences using five of these words.

| change   help   make   parrot |
| pet   second   writer |

1 My dog is my favourite ....
2 This is the .... CD I've got by this singer.
3 Can you .... a cake?
4 He is a brilliant .... of comic books.
5 The weather can .... from hot to cold at night.

2 marks per item: ... / 10 marks

Total: ... / 100

3A I love it!

Vocabulary: school subjects, interests and activities

1 Look at the photos. Complete the words.

a m.*usic*................
b f............................
c t............................
d m............................
e l............................
f a............................
g c............................
h c............................

2 Look at the poster. Write four more activities you can do at the after-school club. Which activity can't you do after school?

GREENWICH AFTER-SCHOOL CLUB

Evening Activities – Monday to Friday

You can do:
..........*cooking*..........

1 ....
2 ....
3 ....
4 ....

You can't do:
5 ....

Come to Our Sports Club!
Saturdays at the Sports Centre
Tel: 0208 504697

3 Find nine more school subjects in the word chain. Write the words.

historymathsartbiologyFrenchgeographyITmusicphysicsEnglish

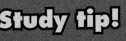

Study tip!

Organise words into categories. It can help you to remember them.

history

1 ....
2 ....
3 ....
4 ....
5 ....
6 ....
7 ....
8 ....
9 ....

4 Complete the table with these words.

basketball   cats   dogs   English
Formula 1   French   hamsters   history
physics   snakes   tennis   volleyball

Animals	School subjects	Sports
....	....	*basketball*
....	....	....
....	....	....
....	....	....

Grammar: present simple (affirmative and negative)

5 Write sentences with *like* or *likes*.

John / basketball
John likes basketball.

1 Molly / shopping

....

2 We / chocolate

....

3 Meg and Tom / heavy metal

....

4 My brother / singing

....

5 Steve and Simon / tennis

....

6 I / snakes

....

7 You / English

....

8 Your sister / school

....

6 Write the sentences in Exercise 5 in the negative form.

John / basketball
John doesn't like basketball.

1 ....
2 ....
3 ....
4 ....
5 ....
6 ....
7 ....
8 ....

7 Write the missing words. Remember to add *-s* at the end of some verbs.

KEY   ☺ = love, ☺ = like, ☺ = not / like, ☹ = hate

1 I ☹ cooking.   ....*hate*......
2 I ☺ reading.   ....
3 I ☺ dancing.   ....
4 I ☹ swimming.   ....
5 You ☹ tennis.   ....
6 We ☺ chocolate.   ....
7 Katie ☺ John.   ....
8 They ☹ Formula 1.   ....
9 He ☺ football.   ....
10 The dog ☹ cats.   ....

8 Write four true sentences with the words.

I	like	rap
My friend	love	snakes
	hate	school
	not like	sleeping
		TV
		pizza

My friend loves pizza.

I hate snakes.

....
....
....
....

Reading

1 Look at the photos. Match the texts (1–3) with the photos (a–c).

a

Justin Timberlake on the golf course

b

Jamie Oliver in his restaurant

c

Alicia Silverstone with her husband

1 I'm married and I live in London. I've got three children, and my wife is a model. I like cooking. I love healthy food and I hate unhealthy food.
Picture: ...*b*....

2 I'm married to singer Christopher Jarecki. We live in Los Angeles. I love animals, especially dogs, and I've got a sanctuary for rescued pets in Los Angeles. I'm a vegan. I love vegetables and I hate meat.
Picture: ....

3 I'm not married but I've got a girlfriend. I live in Hollywood. I'm an actor and a singer. I like dancing and I love playing golf.
Picture: ....

2 Read the sentences. Are they true or false?

		T	F
1	Jamie Oliver is American.	☐	☑
2	Alicia Silverstone is single.	☐	☐
3	Justin Timberlake is married.	☐	☐
4	Alicia Silverstone likes pets.	☐	☐
5	Justin Timberlake likes golf.	☐	☐
6	Jamie Oliver likes fast food.	☐	☐

Listening

3 🔘 **3.1** Listen to the conversation and choose the correct picture.

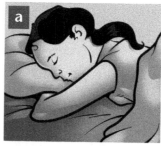
a

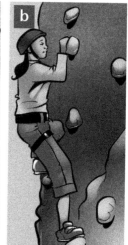
b

c

Grammar: definite article *the*

4 Complete the dialogue. Write *the* or – (no article).

Katie: Let's go to ......*the*........ cinema tonight.

James: Good idea. I like [1]................. adventure films. Do you?

Katie: Yes. I love [2]................. action films too.

James: OK. So, what about *The Dark Knight*?

Katie: What's [3]................. film about?

James: It's [4]................. sequel to *Batman Begins*.

Katie: Who's [5]................. main actor?

James: Christian Bale is [6]................. superhero and Heath Ledger is [7]................. bad guy.

Katie: OK. Sounds good!

5 Read the sentences. Correct the mistakes. Add or cross out *the*.

Look at board.
the

1 Close door.

2 Look at the page 6.

3 What is capital city of France?

4 Put your bag on floor.

5 Helen, what's answer?

Grammar: object pronouns

6 Complete the sentences with object pronouns.

Johnny Depp is fantastic. I love ......*him*........ .

1 My mum can't use the Internet. She doesn't like ....

2 Alicia Silverstone eats vegetables. She eats a lot of ....

3 Look! My friends and I can run fast. Look at ....

4 Anna is ill. What can we send .... ?

5 You don't understand the homework. Ask Jack. He can help ....

3C Eating out

Vocabulary: food

1 Write the items on the menu.

FAST FOOD MENU

beefburger

1 c.......................

2 s.......................

3 a.......................
p.......................

2 Write the names of the food items in the table.

Basket a	Basket b
apples:	....
....	....
....	....
....	....
....	....
....	....
....	....
	....

3 a 🔘 **3.2** Listen to Anna and her mum. Which is their food basket (a or b)?

b Which item in the basket is not mentioned by Anna and her mum?

a

b

4 m.....................

Useful expressions: ordering a meal

4 **Choose the best response for each question.**

1 Can I help you?
   a How much is that?
   b Here you are.
   ©c Can I have a milkshake?
2 Can I have a cheeseburger, please?
   a No, thank you.
   b Of course.
   c Yes, we have.
3 How much is that?
   a Large chips.
   b I'd like a milkshake, please.
   c Six pounds twenty, please.

Pronunciation: *th* and *t*

5 *3.3* **Which three words don't have a /ð/ sound? Listen and circle the words.**

1 mother
2 they
3 potatoes
4 clothes
5 that
6 chemistry
7 this
8 right

Writing: an email

6 **Read the information about Sam. Complete the email to Jacques.**

Penpal information form	
Name	Sam
Age	13
Family	1 sister
Pets	2 cats
Likes & dislikes	films and books – adventure and action stories, <u>not</u> romantic stories
Extra information	favourite actors – Christian Bale, Angelina Jolie
Email address	sam2@ppal.gschool.uk

Dear Jacques,

Hello! My name's ....

....

....

....

....

....

....

....

....

Best wishes,
Sam

Listening and reading

1 Match the words (1–5) with the photos (a–e).

1 a gym ..e......   4 a restaurant ....
2 a kitchen ....   5 a school ....
3 a film ....

2 Match these words with the photos (a–e) in Exercise 1. Some words can go in more than one list.

exercises	director	oil	double IT
action	drink	actor	instructor
burger	physics	sports	teacher

a gym: ....

a kitchen: ....

a film: ....

a restaurant: ....
....

a school: ....

3 Can you add more words to the lists in Exercise 2?

4 🔊 3.4 Look at the pictures (a–e) in Exercise 1. Listen to three recordings. Match one picture with each recording (1–3). You can listen to the recordings twice.

1 ....   2 ....   3 ....

5 Now read the conversations and complete the sentences.

Assistant: Good afternoon. Can I help you?
Girl: Yeah. Can I have a burger and chips, please?
Assistant: Of course. Small or large chips?
Girl: Small, please. And a green salad.
Assistant: Anything to drink?
Girl: Yes. A can of Fanta, please.
Assistant: OK. That's five pounds fifty, please.
Girl: Here you are.

1 The girl orders ....
....

Frank: Look. We've got double IT on Thursday morning.
Jane: Great! I love IT.
Frank: Me too.
Jane: Oh no! We've got physics and chemistry every afternoon. I hate science!
Frank: I don't like physics but chemistry is OK.
Jane: When's history? I like history.
Frank: It's on Tuesday morning. But Mr Morris is the teacher. I don't like him.
Jane: Oh look! We've got art with Mrs Sharpe on Friday morning. I love art and Mrs Sharpe is fantastic!

2 Frank doesn't like .... or
....
Jane loves .... and ....

Mother: Let's make a healthy salad. Look, we can use this cold pasta.
Son: OK. What do we do?
Mother: Well, first you put the pasta in a bowl with some oil.
Son: OK.
Mother: Now we can add tomatoes and tuna.
Son: OK. Can we put in some onion as well? I love onion with tuna.
Mother: Good idea. Anything else?
Son: Yeah. A fork to eat it with!

3 The ingredients for the pasta salad are pasta, oil, ...
....

Reading

6 Complete the words to name some national dishes.

b <u>i g o s</u>

s _ _ _ h e t t i

p a _ _ l a

c _ _ r y

f i _ _ a _ d c _ _ _ s

h a _ _ _ r g e r

7 Write the name of the dishes next to the countries they come from.

country	food
Poland	.... *bigos* ....
India	....
Spain	....
the USA	....
the UK	....
Italy	....

8 Read the advertisement for Julio's restaurant. <u>Underline</u> four food items and dishes you can eat there. Write them here.

1 ....

2 ....

3 ....

4 ....

9 Read the advertisement again and answer these questions with short answers.

1 Is Julio's a French restaurant?

....

2 Are the salad ingredients from the market?

....

3 Are the cheeses from Italy?

....

4 Can you have lunch in the garden in winter?

....

5 Is the restaurant in Manchester?

....

10 Read the advertisement again and decide which sentences (1–5) are true and which are false.

	T	F
1 Julio's is an Italian restaurant.	☐	☐
2 The salad ingredients are from the garden.	☐	☐
3 The cheeses are from France.	☐	☐
4 You can have lunch in the garden in summer.	☐	☐
5 The restaurant is in London.	☐	☐

Julio's Restaurant

The Best Italian Food in Town!
Everybody loves our pasta dishes!
We make fresh salads with ingredients from our vegetable garden.
Large selection of Italian cheeses.
And our pizzas are famous!
We serve lunches in the garden in the summer.
Come to Julio's!
12 South Parade, Manchester.

Grammar Practice Unit 3

present simple (affirmative and negative)

We use the **present simple** to talk about things that are always true, things we do often or that happen often, etc.

*It **snows** in winter.*

*You **speak** Spanish very well.*

*I **play** football every Wednesday.*

In the affirmative, we add -s to the verb after he, *she* or *it*.

I/You/We/They <u>like</u> football.   He/She/It <u>likes</u> football.

> With verbs that end in **-ss**, **-sh**, **-ch**, **-x** and **-o**, we add **-es**.
>
> mi**ss**es   wa**sh**es   wat**ch**es   fi**x**es   go**es**
>
> With verbs that end in a consonant + **-y**, we change the **-y** to **-ies**.
>
> stu**dy**   studies   car**ry**   carries

In the negative, we use **do not** or **does not** and the bare infinitive of the main verb. We DON'T add –s or –es to the main verb.

The short form is **don't** or **doesn't**.

*I **don't like** history.*

*Ivan **doesn't speak** Spanish.*

Affirmative		
I/You/We/They He/She/It	like/love/hate likes/loves/hates	rock music.
Negative		
I/You/We/They He/She/It	don't (do not) doesn't (does not)	like	rap music.

1 Put the words in the correct order to make sentences.

love / I / animals

I love animals.

1 sports / hates / Harry

....

2 Claude / languages / likes

....

3 fashion / Anna and Meera / love

....

4 hate / we / snakes

....

5 love / rap music / they

....

2 Complete the sentences with *like/likes* (✔) or *hate/hates* (✘).

Karen and John .....*like*..... adventure films. (✔)

1 He really .... heavy metal. (✘)

2 I .... pizza. (✔)

3 They .... biology. (✔)

4 You .... tennis. (✘)

5 Jeanne .... fashion. (✔)

6 We .... basketball. (✔)

3 Complete the sentences with the correct form of the verb.

Myra ....*studies*........ art history. (**study**)

1 He often .... shopping. (**go**)

2 Ben .... tennis very well. (**play**)

3 She .... TV every night. (**watch**)

4 Complete the sentences with *don't* or *doesn't*.

Michael ......*doesn't*...... like geography.

1 We .... like comics.

2 Girls .... usually like spiders.

3 Jeanne .... like physics or IT.

4 Judy and Helen .... like films.

5 I .... like fashion.

5 Write sentences with these words. Use short forms.

I / not like / fast food / but I / like / ice-cream

I don't like fast food but I like ice-cream.

1 some people / not like / chocolate

....

2 he / like / animals / but he / not like /snakes

....

3 Angela / not like / tennis or basketball

....

4 my brother and I / not like / cats

....

5 they / not like / heavy metal / but they / love / rap.

....

like/love/hate + nouns & -ing words

After **(don't) like**, **love** and **hate**, we can use nouns (*books, music, etc*) or -ing words.

*I **like** <u>films</u>. I also **like** <u>reading</u>.*

*My brother **doesn't like** <u>fashion</u> and he **hates** <u>shopping</u>.*

*We **love** <u>food</u> but we **don't like** <u>cooking</u>.*

6 Write sentences with these words. Use short forms.

KEY:	😍 love	😊 like	😐 don't like	😠 hate

Jack - / 😊 cycling / 😐 animals
Jack likes cycling but he doesn't like animals.

1 Mark - / 😐 music / 😍 dancing

....

2 Emma and Alan - / 😊 reading / 😍 comics

....

3 Pablo - / 😊 sports / 😍 swimming

....

4 Lucia - / 😊 painting / 😐 cooking

....

5 Will - / 😊 sleeping / 😐 singing

....

6 Erica - / 😍 food / 😍 cooking

....

definite article *the*

We use **the** to talk about a specific thing or group. It is specific because:

* there is only one *(the Earth, the Moon, the sky, etc)*

The Moon goes around the Earth.

* we explain, describe or understand clearly which one we mean

The boy next door is my friend. (Which boy? The boy next door.)

That's my mobile – the blue one. (Which one? The blue one.)

This is a good film. The actors are very funny. (Which actors? The actors in this film.)

We don't normally use **the** for names, cities, countries, etc.

~~the~~ Brad, ~~the~~ New Delhi, ~~the~~ Spain, ~~the~~ Africa

> BUT: **the** UK, **the** USA
> We use **the** for times of day:
> in **the** morning   in **the** afternoon
> in **the** evening
> BUT: at ~~the~~ night

7 Complete the text with *the* or – (no article).

........–...... Greenwich is in (**1**) .... London, (**2**) .... capital city of (**3**) .... UK. (**4**) ...... Greenwich meridian is (**5**) .... 'line' between east and west. (**6**) .... USA is west of (**7**) .... line. When it's midday in (**8**) .... London, it's seven o'clock in (**9**) .... morning in (**10**) .... New York. In (**11**) .... India, it's five o'clock in (**12**) .... afternoon. In (**13**) .... Sydney, (**14**) .... Australia, it's ten o'clock at (**15**) .... night.

object pronouns

We can use **object pronouns** after the main verb.
*I can't do this. Can you <u>help</u> **me**, please?*
*Are you in this photograph? I can't <u>see</u> **you**.*
*Brad is my cousin. You <u>know</u> **him**.*
*That girl is in my class, but I don't <u>like</u> **her**.*
*I can't find my book. Can you <u>see</u> **it**?*
*We can dance really well. <u>Watch</u> **us**!*
*They are my sweets – don't <u>eat</u> **them**!*

Subject pronouns							
I	you	he	she	it	we	you	they
Object pronouns							
me	you	him	her	it	us	you	them

8 Write the object pronouns for the <u>underlined</u> words.

That dog bites! Don't touch <u>the dog</u>!
   it ....

1 They're my friends. I like playing with <u>my friends</u>.

   ....

2 Andrew and I like him, but he doesn't speak to <u>Andrew and me</u>.

   ....

3 Meera's my best friend. I really like <u>Meera</u>.

   ....

4 This is my computer. I've got lots of games on <u>my computer</u>.

   ....

5 Harry's over there. Let's speak to <u>Harry</u>.

   ....

6 Is this your pencil? Can I borrow <u>your pencil</u>?

   ....

9 Complete the sentences with object pronouns.

Is that your sister? I don't know ....*her*........ .

1 You've got a problem. Can I help .... ?
2 He doesn't like school. Actually, he hates .... !
3 They're my comics. I like collecting ....
4 We like going to the cinema. Come with .... tonight.
5 I'm not her friend. She doesn't like ....
6 He's very tall. Look at .... !

4A Do you like sports?

Vocabulary: sports

1 Find ten more sports in the word square.
Write the words.

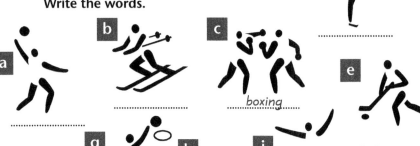

boxing

B	O	X	I	N	G	T	O	P	T
X	A	T	H	L	E	T	I	C	S
H	W	S	M	P	S	K	N	T	F
O	D	R	K	J	K	W	F	E	O
C	T	I	D	E	A	S	F	N	O
K	Q	R	V	Y	T	I	E	N	T
E	H	U	B	I	I	B	S	I	B
Y	S	K	I	I	N	G	A	S	A
K	G	T	D	J	G	G	E	L	L
V	O	L	L	E	Y	B	A	L	L
G	Y	M	N	A	S	T	I	C	S

2 Complete the lists with the words from Exercise 1.
Some words can go in more than one list.

Indoor sports: _basketball_

Outdoor sports: _football_

Sports with balls:

Sports for two people:

Sports for two teams:

Sports for individuals:

3 Write your daily routine. Use the verbs in box A
and the words in box B.

A		B	
arrive	have	a bath	my homework
brush	have	a shower	lunch
do	have	breakfast	the house
~~get~~	have	dinner	to bed
get	have	dressed	your teeth
go	leave	home	~~up~~

1 get up
2
3
4
5
6
7
8
9
10
11
12

4 Look at the pictures. Complete the text.

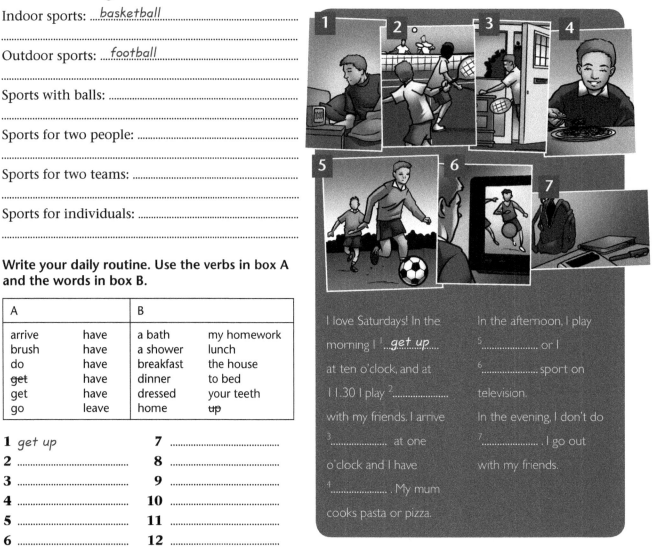

I love Saturdays! In the morning I ¹ _get up_ at ten o'clock, and at 11.30 I play ² .... with my friends. I arrive ³ .... at one o'clock and I have ⁴ .... My mum cooks pasta or pizza.

In the afternoon, I play ⁵ .... or I ⁶ .... sport on television.

In the evening, I don't do ⁷ .... I go out with my friends.

Grammar: present simple (questions and short answers)

5 Circle *Do* or *Does*. Then write short answers to the questions.

(Do)/ Does you support Liverpool? (✔)
...... Yes, I do. ......

1 *Do / Does* Sally play hockey? (✘)
....

2 *Do / Does* you and your friends like skating? (✔) ....

3 *Do / Does* we go to school on Sundays? (✘)
....

4 *Do / Does* your dad go to football matches? (✔) ....

5 *Do / Does* the match start at 2 o'clock? (✘)
....

Grammar: questions with *Wh-* words

6 Circle the correct option.

(What time)/ What do you get up?

1 *Where / What* do you have for breakfast?
2 *When / Where* does your dad leave the house?
3 *What / When* do your friends do at the weekend?
4 *Where / When* do your grandparents live?
5 *Where / What time* does school finish?

7 Read about Helen. Then write the questions for her answers.

Where are you from? ....
Nottingham.

1 ....
In the city centre.

2 ....
At nine o'clock.

3 ....
On Wednesdays.

4 ....
I do gymnastics.

5 ....
On Sundays.

Helen is from Nottingham, in England. She goes to school in the city centre. School starts at nine o'clock. She plays basketball on Wednesdays after school. On Saturdays she does gymnastics and, on Sundays, she visits her grandparents.

Reading

1 Complete the table with these words.

> author coach cycle dollars doubles
> favourite actress listen to music matches
> pet rat practise prize read routine run win

Free time	Competitions	Training

2 Read the text and choose the best heading from Exercise 1 for each paragraph.

Study tip!

Underline the answers in the text.

AGNIESZKA RADWAŃSKA – TENNIS STAR

1 ....

Agnieszka Radwańska is from Kraków in Poland. She's a young tennis player but she plays in international matches and Grand Slam competitions. She wins lots of prizes and trophies. She is the first Polish woman tennis player to win more than one million dollars.

2 ....

She has a training routine for each competition. She practises every morning for three hours. She trains in the gym and she runs and cycles. Her father is her coach and he helps her. She often trains with her sister, Urszula. She is a tennis player too. They play in doubles competitions and they often win.

3 Match the questions (1–7) with the answers (a–g).

1 Where is Agnieszka from?
2 When does she practise?
3 What does Agnieszka win?
4 Does she win a lot of money?
5 Does she play in competitions with her sister?
6 What does she do in her free time?
7 What is her favourite city?

a She reads books and listens to music.
b Prizes and trophies.
c Paris.
d Every morning, for three hours.
e Kraków, Poland.
f Yes, she does. They play doubles.
g Yes, she does.

4 Are these sentences true or false?

	T	F
1 Agnieszka has got one million dollars.	✔	
2 She trains with her father and her sister.		
3 Every morning she runs and swims.		
4 Agnieszka has got a dog and a cat.		
5 Her favourite writer is Dorota Terakowska.		

3 ....
Agnieszka has got two pet rats named Flippy and Floppy. Her favourite actress is Nicole Kidman and she loves Paris. In her free time, she enjoys listening to music, especially Green Day, Black Eyed Peas and Eminem. She also likes reading books and her favourite author is Dorota Terakowska.

Listening

5 💿 **4.1** **Listen to the conversation and choose the correct sport.**

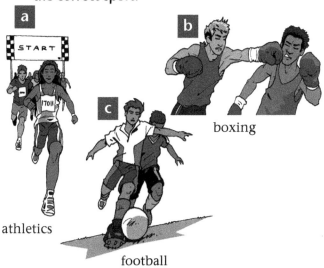

athletics

a
START

b
boxing

c
football

6 💿 **4.1** **Listen again and choose the correct option (a, b or c).**

1 When does Tim go to the gym?
  a On Saturdays.
  b Three times a week.
  c Every day.

2 Where do the team usually train?
  a Outdoors.
  b In the gym.
  c In a match.

3 Do the team win their matches?
  a Yes, they sometimes win.
  b No, they never win.
  c Yes, they usually win.

Grammar: adverbs of frequency

7 **Put the adverbs in the correct place.**

I have fruit for breakfast. (always)
I always have fruit for breakfast.

1 Rachel is late for school. (sometimes)

....

2 We go to the cinema at the weekend. (usually)

....

3 My brother helps me with my homework. (often)

....

4 My grandparents are happy. (always)

....

5 My grandfather cooks the dinner! (never)

....

8 **Put the words in the correct order.**

runs / often / Tim / in the morning
Tim often runs in the morning.

1 the team / play in a match / usually / on Saturdays

....

2 play in a match / they / on Sundays / sometimes

....

3 with their coach / train / the team / often

....

4 at the weekend / never / lose / they / their matches

....

Vocabulary: time

1 **Write the time under each clock.**

It`s seven o'clock.

1 It's ....
....

2 ....
....

3 ....
....

4 ....
....

5 ....
....

Vocabulary: daily routine

2 **Match the verbs (1–10) with the expressions (a–j).**

1 get up		**a**	with your family
2 play		**b**	a book
3 perform		**c**	a medal
4 win		**d**	lunch in a restaurant
5 have		**e**	late
6 go		**f**	in a competition
7 relax		**g**	tennis
8 train		**h**	to the gym
9 read		**i**	to the library
10 go		**j**	for two hours

3 **a** **Complete the texts. Use the verbs in Exercise 2.**

a

b

Picture
....

I love sport and I'm a skater. At the weekend, I ....*train*........... for two hours each day. On Saturdays, I usually ^{1}................................ in a competition. I always ^{2}................................ a medal. On Sundays, I ^{3}................................ to the gym or ^{4}................................ tennis.

Picture
....

I hate sport. At the weekend, I ^{5}................................ late and ^{6}................................ a book for two or three hours. On Saturdays I usually ^{7}................................ to the library. On Sundays, I ^{8}................................ with my family and we sometimes ^{9}................................ lunch in a restaurant.

b **Which picture (a or b) goes with which text?**

4 Join these sentences with *and* or *but*.

My sister plays tennis. She doesn't play hockey.
My sister plays tennis but she doesn't play hockey.

1 John goes to bed late. He gets up late.

....

2 I like tennis. I don't play in competitions.

....

3 Jill goes to the gym every day. She trains for two hours.

....

4 My dad doesn't play football. He watches it on TV.

....

Pronunciation: sounds with /ɜː/

5 🔊 **4.2** **Listen to these words. Repeat.**

burger	circus	first	girl	her	hurt	learn
purse	third	turn	world	work		

Writing: free time

6 **What do you do in your free time? Write sentences. Use the adverbs in the box.**

often	usually	never

After school

I usually practise the piano.

1 ....

2 ....

3 ....

At weekends

I often visit my grandparents.

4 ....

5 ....

6 ....

7 **Write two things you *don't* do in your free time.**

I never get up early on Sundays.

1 ....

2 ....

8 a **Read this email from Patricia about her free time.**

: *File*   Edit   *View*   Insert   *Format*   *Tools*   *Table*

To... debbiesmith21@mymail.com
From... pattiredhair@dotmail.com
Send   Sent...
Subject... my free time

Hi Debbie,

Thanks for your email. I like the photo of you with your swimming medals! So, what do I do in my free time?

Well, after school, I usually practise the piano and do my homework. We usually have dinner about six o'clock. After dinner, I often watch TV or use the Internet. On Thursdays, I sometimes go to the cinema with my friends but we always come home early. On Fridays, I sometimes do my homework.

At the weekend, I often go to the gym or play tennis. On Sundays, I get up late. In the afternoon, we usually visit my grandparents. I always practise the piano and do homework on Sunday evening.

Best wishes

Patricia

b **Now write an email to a friend. Say what you do in your free time. Use *and* and *but*.**

....

....

....

....

....

....

....

....

....

....

Reading

1 Put these activities into a logical order.

a have breakfast   **d** go home
b get up   **e** do sport outdoors
c leave the house

1 .... 2 .... 3 .... 4 .... 5 ....

2 Read the photo story and put the pictures in a logical order. Choose the correct answer (A, B or C).

A d, b, a, c, e
B d, a, b, c, e
C d, a, b, e, c

Paula always gets up early and prepares her bag.

Sometimes the matches are in another city and she goes on the team bus.

She has breakfast and her dad drives her to the sports club.

Paula Redman is fourteen years old. Every Saturday she plays hockey for her team.

Her team often wins the match and Paula is very happy when she gets home.

3 Put the sentences in the correct order. Choose the correct answer (A, B or C).

a David is in a school show. He practises very hard and he's very good.
b David Williams can sing and dance. He's thirteen years old and he lives in Wales.
c David asks his mum, 'What do you think?' She says it's a great opportunity.
d David and his mum go to London for six months and David performs in a big musical.
e A famous musical director sees the show and asks David to go to London. David thinks, 'Wow! This is fantastic.'

A a, c, b, e, d
B d, b, a, c, d
C b, a, e, c, d

4 **Complete the texts about David's life in London with the verbs.**

| be | go | live |

David now [1].. in a flat in West London with his mum. It [2].. a very small flat. They don't [3].. home to Wales at weekends.

| finish | practise | work |

After lunch, David and the other singers and actors [10].. for the show. They [11].. really hard. They usually [12].. at five o'clock in the evening.

| arrive | go | leave |

Life as a young actor is very difficult. David [4].. home early every morning and [5].. to the theatre on the London Underground. He never [6].. late.

| arrive | cook | do |

David usually [13].. home about 6.30 and his mum [14].. their dinner. Then he [15].. his homework in his bedroom.

David [7].. singing and dancing classes every morning at half past eight. He can sing but he [8].. dance. The class [9].. very difficult.

| be | can | have |

Grammar Practice Unit 4

present simple (questions and short answers)

We make questions by putting **do** or **does** before the subject, and then the bare infinitive of the main verb. We DON'T add *–s* or *–es* to the main verb.

Do you **like** football?
Does she **go** to your school?
Does it **rain** a lot here?

In short answers, we don't use the main verb.
Does she live in New York? – Yes, she **does***.*
Do they study physics? – No, they **don't***.*

Questions		
Do Does	I/you/we/they he/she/it	play computer games?
Short answers		
Yes, Yes,	I/you/we/they Yes, he/she/it	do. does.	No, No,	I/you/we/they he/she/it	don't. doesn't.

1 Complete the questions with *do* or *does*.

................*Do*................ you like football?
1 .... Brad play hockey?
2 .... we learn English?
3 .... I know you?
4 .... our lesson start at 11 a.m.?
5 .... you and Simon do gymnastics?
6 .... your friends support Barcelona?
7 .... Teresa go to school with you?

2 Write questions from these sentences.

Daniel collects model aeroplanes.
Does Daniel collect model aeroplanes?
1 She goes swimming every day.
....
2 That parrot speaks.
....
3 I play tennis every Wednesday.
....
4 You like watching basketball.
....
5 They live in Argentina.
....
6 My best friend loves skiing.
....

3 Choose the correct short answers to these questions.

Do you watch TV every night?
A Yes, I watch.   **B** Yes, I do watch.   **(C)** Yes, I do.
1 Do they play American football?
   A No, they don't.
   B No, they doesn't.
   C No, they don't like.
2 Does Harry like watching basketball?
   A Yes, he does like.
   B Yes, he does.
   C Yes, he likes.
3 Do we go to school on Fridays?
   A Yes, we do go.
   B Yes, we go.
   C Yes, we do.
4 Does your friend go swimming on Mondays?
   A No, she doesn't go.
   B No, she doesn't.
   C No, she don't.
5 Do I play computer games every day?
   A Yes, you do.
   B Yes, you do play.
   C Yes, you play.

4 Put the words in the correct order to make questions.

go / Harry's dad / to the match / does / every Saturday?
Does Harry's dad go to the match every Saturday?
1 does / go / Harry / to bed late?
....
2 do / does / her homework / Sally / every day?
....
3 skating / James and Kim / do / watch / on TV?
....
4 Julia / speak / does / French?
....
5 live / your best friends / do / in your street?
....

5 Now write affirmative (✔) or negative (✘) short answers to the questions in Exercise 4.

(Does Harry's dad go to the match every Saturday?)
(✔) ....*Yes, he does.*................
1 ✘ ....
2 ✔ ....
3 ✔ ....
4 ✘ ....
5 ✔ ....

questions with Wh- words

We use **question words** when we want more information than *yes* or *no*.

We begin with the question word, followed by *do/does* or *am/are/is*.

What *does she play? – The piano.*
What *is your name? – Miriam.*
When *do you play football? – On Saturdays.*
When *is my next English lesson? – On Wednesday.*
What *time does the film start? – At 6 o'clock.*
What *time is it? – 6 o'clock.*
Where *do you live? – In South Street.*
Where *is my mobile? – In the kitchen.*

6 Choose the correct question words to complete these questions.

.... do you like watching on TV?
A Where   **(B)** What   **C** When

1 .... are you from?
   A Where   **B** What   **C** When

2 .... do you want for lunch?
   A When   **B** What time   **C** What

3 .... do you go to bed?
   A Where   **B** What time   **C** What

4 .... is your birthday?
   A Where   **B** What   **C** When

5 .... does your friend live?
   A Where   **B** What   **C** When

7 Put the words in the correct order to make questions.

do / what / you / do / on Sundays?
What do you do on Sundays?

1 you / what / eat / do / for breakfast?
....

2 they / go / do / where / skiing?
....

3 go / does / she / when / swimming?
....

4 time / what / the film / does / finish?
....

5 Harry's / do / grandparents / where / live?
....

8 Write questions for these answers.

.......*What time does the match start?*.......
The match starts <u>at 4.00 p.m.</u>

1 ....?
   I collect <u>toy cars</u>.

2 ....?
   Sally's book is <u>in her schoolbag</u>.

3 ....?
   My parents get up <u>at 7.00 a.m.</u>

4 ....?
   We like playing <u>tennis</u>.

5 ....?
   Basketball practice is <u>on Thursday</u>.

adverbs of frequency

We use **adverbs of frequency** to talk about habits or how often something happens.

100% ◄─────────────────────► 0%
always   usually   often   sometimes   never

> Adverbs of frequency go before the main verb.
> *She **often** <u>goes</u> swimming.*
> *They **always** <u>have</u> lunch at 1 o'clock.*
> **BUT** they go after the verb ***be***.
> *It <u>is</u> **usually** warm in the summer.*
> *We <u>are</u> **never** at school on Saturdays.*

9 Put the adverbs in the correct place.

I go to football practice on Wednesdays. (**usually**)
I usually go to football practice on Wednesdays.

1 Harry is late for school. (**often**)
....

2 We watch boxing on TV. (**never**)
....

3 Karen is in bed at 10.00 p.m. (**usually**)
....

4 I cycle to school. (**always**)
....

5 My parents go to the cinema in the evening. (**sometimes**)
....

10 Put the words in the correct order to make sentences.

its matches / never / wins / my team
My team never wins its matches.

1 go / sometimes / I / with my mother / shopping
....

2 I / eat / for breakfast / usually / cereal
....

3 are / the players / after a match / tired / always
....

4 never / for swimming training / is / Karim / late
....

5 after school / with my friends / often / I / play
....

Review Units 3 and 4

1 Complete the sentences with the correct form of the verbs.

1 Peter .... fashion and shopping. (love)
2 Jessica is vegetarian and................ meat. (not/eat)
3 Simone .... in Paris. (live)
4 My sisters .... basketball. (not/like)
5 My dad .... to work every day. (cycle)

1 mark per item: ... / 5 marks

2 Complete the sentences with *the* or – (no article).

1 Look at .... camera. Smile!
2 Steven likes walking by .... River Thames.
3 Madonna is .... singer of that famous song.
4 Wayne doesn't like .... Manchester United.
5 We love swimming in .... sea.

1 mark per item: ... / 5 marks

3 Complete the sentences with the correct object pronouns.

1 Look at those people. Do you know ....?
2 Where are your comics? Did you bring ....?
3 Do you see that man? Give the keys to ....
4 Do you know Clare? Do you go to school with ....?
5 I've got a new film on DVD. I really like ....

1 mark per item: ... / 5 marks

4 Complete the questions and short answers with *do, does, don't* or *doesn't*.

1 .... your dad drive to work at 8 a.m.?
   Yes, he ....
2 .... Ben and Vicky cycle every weekend?
   No, they ....
3 .... you listen to your teacher?
   Yes, I ....
4 .... you and your cousin play computer games?
   No, we ....
5 .... your parents cook your dinner?
   Yes, they ....

2 marks per item: ... / 10 marks

5 Complete the questions with *do* or *does*.

1 .... Jenny like skating?
2 .... you play basketball?
3 .... they go swimming every weekend?
4 .... she go to school on Saturdays?
5 .... Harry and Tim love football?

1 mark per item: ... / 5 marks

6 Choose the correct words.

1 I *have usually / usually have* a sandwich for lunch.
2 We *always are / are always* on time for football matches.
3 They *sometimes go / go sometimes* to the cinema.
4 Sandy *usually gets / gets usually* to work at 9.30 a.m.
5 My sister *often is / is often* late for school.

1 mark per item: ... / 5 marks

7 Write sentences with the verb in the present simple.

1 he/do/his homework/never.
   ....
2 be/often/Diane/at the library.
   ....
3 go/sometimes/they/to the beach.
   ....
4 Joseph/usually/to school/cycle.
   ....
5 go/never/to the cinema/my parents.
   ....

1 mark per item: ... / 5 marks

8 Write questions to the answers using these words.

What	What time	When	Where

1 Daniel usually goes swimming on Thursdays.
   ....
2 Steve and Mary are from New York in the USA.
   ....
3 She likes cheese in her sandwiches.
   ....
4 School starts at nine o'clock every morning.
   ....
5 They always study at the library.
   ....

2 marks per item: ... / 10 marks

9 Complete the sentences with the school subjects.

art   biology   French   IT   music

1 She likes .... She's got a guitar.
2 I can draw pictures. I like ....
3 She likes languages. Her favourite subject is
  ....
4 He's good with computers. He likes ....
5 I don't like .... I'm not good at science.

1 mark per item: ... / 5 marks

10 Write the interests.

cooking   dancing   drawing
shopping   sleeping

1 Mary likes .... pictures.
2 I don't like getting out of bed. I like ....
3 My brother likes .... pasta.
4 She loves .... to hip-hop music.
5 We like .... We spend a lot of money
  on clothes.

1 mark per item: ... / 5 marks

11 Complete the sentences using these words.

cheeseburger   chips   milkshake
salad   vegetarian

1 Can I have a double .... and chips?
2 I'd like a green ...., please.
3 A sandwich and a chocolate ...., please.
4 Can I have large ....?
5 I don't eat meat. Can I have a .... burger,
  please?

1 mark per item: ... / 5 marks

12 Fill in the gaps using five of these words.

animals   basketball   favourite   food
hate   physics   reading

My name is Fiona. My favourite subject is
(1)................. . I love cooking. My favourite
(2)................. is pizza. I don't like (3).................,
except comics. I love films. My (4)................. film
is Planet 51. I've got two cats and a parrot.
I love (5)................. .

2 marks per item: ... / 10 marks

13 Match the sentences with the sports.

1 I like a sport that needs   a tennis
  two wheels.   b cycling
2 I like a sport on snow.   c football
3 I like a sport on ice.   d skating
4 I like a sport with two teams.   e skiing
5 I like a sport with two or
  four players.

1 mark per item: ... / 5 marks

14 Complete the sentences with these words.

arrive   do   go   have   play

1 I .... home from school at 4 o'clock.
2 I .... football after school.
3 I .... a shower after football.
4 I .... my homework before I sleep.
5 I .... to bed at 10 p.m. every night.

1 mark per item: ... / 5 marks

15 Choose the correct words.

1 The football game **starts/plays** at 3.00 p.m.
2 Jimmy **sees/watches** athletics every summer.
3 Kate and Sally **go/do** swimming every
  Tuesday evening.
4 Does your teacher **live/leave** in your town?
5 What does he **like/want** for his birthday?

1 mark per item: ... / 5 marks

16 Complete the sentences with five of these words.

arrive   get   go   have
leave   practise   wake up

1 I .... the house at 8:30 every morning.
2 I .... the piano with my music teacher.
3 I .... dressed after breakfast.
4 I .... dinner at six o'clock every evening.
5 I .... and go to school in the morning.

2 marks per item: ... / 10 marks

Total: ... / 100

5A Home sweet home

Vocabulary: natural features

1 **Label the natural features. Use these words.**

> ~~beach~~   desert   field   ~~ice~~   lake   mountain
> path   river   sea   snow   tree

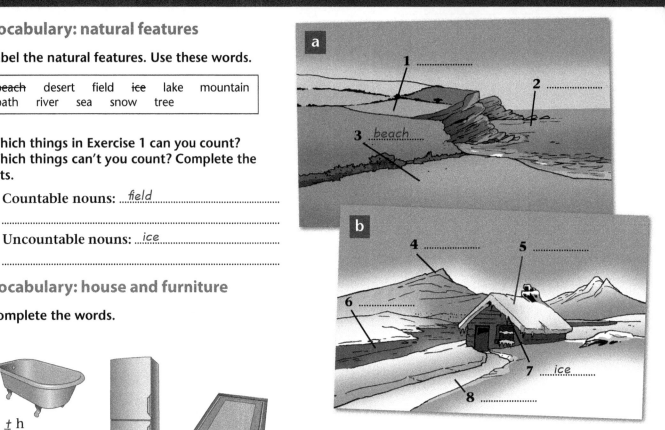

a

1 ....

2 ....

3 *beach*

2 **Which things in Exercise 1 can you count? Which things can't you count? Complete the lists.**

1 Countable nouns: ...*field*...................................

....

2 Uncountable nouns: ...*ice*...............................

....

b

4 ....

5 ....

6 ....

7 ...*ice*...............

8 ....

Vocabulary: house and furniture

3 **Complete the words.**

b <u>a</u> <u>t</u> h

1 f _ _ d _ _

2 _ _ g

3 w _ _ _ _ g
m _ _ _ _ e

4 c _ _ b _ _ _ d

5 d _ _ _ w _ _ _ _ r

6 c _ _ _ t _ f
d _ _ w _ _ s

7 s _ _ _ _ r

8 s _ _ _ _ _ s

9 m _ _ _ _ w _ _ _

10 w _ _ _ _ _ _ e

4 **Look at the plan of the house. Label the rooms.**

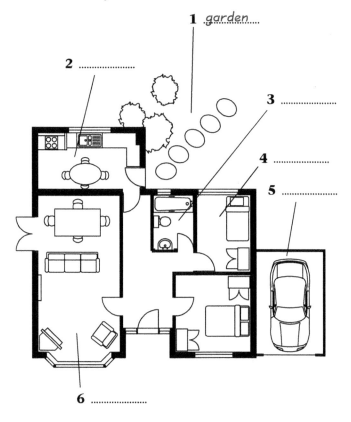

1 *garden*

2 ....

3 ....

4 ....

5 ....

6 ....

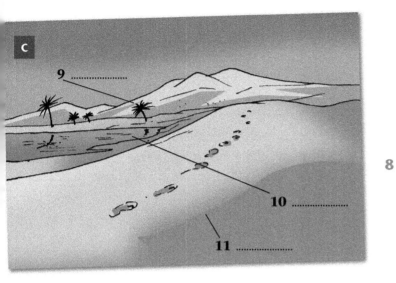

c

9 ....

10 ....

11 ....

5 Tick (✔) the rooms where you find these things.

	bedroom	living room	study	garage	bathroom	kitchen
rug	✔	✔	✔		✔	✔
sofa						
wardrobe						
car						
washing machine						
shower						
microwave						
desk and chair						
bed						
computer						

6 Are the sentences true or false?

		T	F
1	You put cheese, milk, salad and cold drinks in the fridge.	✔	☐
2	You put books in a chest of drawers.	☐	☐
3	You can wash clothes in a dishwasher.	☐	☐
4	Ceiling lights are next to the bed.	☐	☐
5	You can see cupboards in every room of the house.	☐	☐

Grammar: present continuous (affirmative and negative)

7 **Complete the sentences with the present continuous affirmative form of these verbs.**

~~have~~ make run study swim write

John *is having* a shower.

1 Mary and Sally .... in the library.

2 Rebecca .... in the pool.

3 I .... an email to my friend.

4 The athletes .... in a race.

5 My mum .... a birthday cake.

8 **Correct the sentences. Write one sentence with the negative form and one with the affirmative form.**

John is having a bath.

John isn't having a bath. He's reading a book.

Ann and Helen are using the computer.

1 ....
....
....

Dad is washing the clothes.

2 ....
....
....

The boys are doing their homework.

3 ....
....
....

The dog is eating its dinner.

4 ....
....
....

The people are singing.

5 ....
....
....

9 **Complete the text with the present continuous form of the verbs.**

It's Sunday afternoon. Mum .....*is reading*..............
(read) the newspaper in the living room. Dad
[1]... (not relax) in the living room. He
[2]... (make) a cake in the kitchen. Mike
and Tom [3]... (play) computer games
in their bedroom. Linda [4]... (not do)
her homework. She [5]... (practise) the
piano. The cats [6]... (sleep).

Grammar: present continuous (questions and short answers)

1 Look at the pictures. Write questions with the present continuous form and short answers. Then write affirmative sentences.

the birds / dance / fight
Are the birds dancing?
No, they aren't. They're fighting.

1 the students / sleep / study

....

2 the fish / fly / jump

....

3 the girl / phone her friend / take a photo

....

2 Write questions with the present continuous form. Then write short answers.

she / write / an email (✔)
Is she writing an email? Yes, she is.

1 he / play / the piano? (✗)

....

2 it / rain? (✔)

....

3 they / play / basketball? (✗)

....

4 we / study? (✔)

....

5 she / make / lunch? (✗)

....

3 Read the sentences. Correct the mistakes.

Penelope writting to her aunt.
Penelope is writing to her aunt.

1 We are having pizza for dinner?

....

2 My sister are doing her homework.

....

3 Do you making a cake?

....

4 The boys is playing football outdoors.

....

5 I aren't playing computer games. I'm working!

....

6 Is your mum watching TV? Yes, she's.

....

Reading and listening

4 Match these words with the headings and complete the table. Some words can go in both columns.

~~bears~~   cabins   crocodiles   fish   ice
Indians   the Inuits   mountains   parrots
polar   river   sea   snakes   snow   trees

The Amazon	The Arctic
....	*bears*
....	....
....	....
....	....
....	....
....	....
....	....
....	....

5 ◎**5.1** **Read and listen to the radio programme. Choose the best photo (a or b) for the text.**

a Travelling up the Amazon

b Travelling on the Arctic sea

Presenter (Mark): Good morning and welcome to *Natural World*. Today we are talking to Samantha King in the Amazon and John Greene in the Arctic. First, let's go to Samantha. Samantha. Hello. Where are you?

Samantha: At the moment, I'm travelling up the river on a small boat. There are two native Indians with me. It's evening and it's getting dark, but I can see the crocodiles. They're sleeping by the river. Oh! There are hundreds of green birds above our heads – I think they're parrots! They're flying to a big tree. Can you hear them?

Mark: No, sorry we can't. What …

Samantha: What's that?! Something's hitting the boat! They're fish! They're jumping out of the water and into the boat! I think we can have fish for supper tonight! Oh … I think we're stopping. I can't talk now.

Mark: OK. Thanks very much, Samantha.

6 **Are the sentences true or false?**

	T	F
There are four Indians in the boat.	☐	✔
1 The crocodiles are sleeping by the river.	☐	☐
2 A crocodile is hitting the boat.	☐	☐
3 The fish are jumping out of the boat.	☐	☐
4 Samantha and the Indians can eat the fish.	☐	☐

Grammar: *there is/are* **with** *a, some, any*

7 **Complete the sentences. Circle the correct word.**

There is *a* / *an* / *(some)* cheese in the fridge.

1 There is *a* / *some* clock on the wall.

2 There are *a* / *some* biscuits in the cupboard.

3 There is *an* / *some* / *a* orange in a bowl.

8 **Look at the photo of the Arctic in Exercise 5. Write questions and answers.**

(boats) *Are there any boats?*

Yes, there are some boats.

1 (snow) ....

2 (trees) ....

3 (mountains) ....

4 (ice) ....

5 (water) ....

Listening

9 **What do you imagine is inside an igloo? Put a tick (✔) or a cross (✗) next to these things.**

a big kitchen and living room ✔

1 sofas and chairs   **5** a television

2 a fire   **6** newspapers

3 pictures   **7** a bedroom

4 rugs

10 ◎**5.2** **Listen to John Greene in the Arctic and check your answers to Exercise 9.**

11 ◎**5.2** **Listen again. Circle the correct option.**

John is in *(Canada)* / *Alaska* with a family of Inuits.

1 He's having *breakfast* / *tea* with the family.

2 Their grandmother *is cooking* / *is watching TV*.

3 Mark is sitting on *ice* / *a chair*.

4 There are *pictures* / *newspapers* on the walls.

1 Complete the dialogues. Put the words in the correct order.

Dialogue 1

A: my / go / let's / house / to

....

B: That's a great idea.

A: swim / our / in / can / pool / we

....

B: OK. I love swimming.

Dialogue 2

A: It's Uncle Steve's birthday today.

B: we / him / phone / on / webcam? / why / the / don't

....

A: That's a good idea.

B: sing / Happy / to / Birthday / him / can / we

....

Dialogue 3

A: Why / basketball / go / to / the / we / game? / don't

....

B: Sorry, but I don't like basketball. It's boring.

A: go / the / we / cinema / to / instead / can

....

B: Good idea.

2 a Mike and Sandra are organising a birthday celebration for their friend, Meera. Match the sentence beginnings (1–6) with the endings (a–f) to complete their suggestions.

1 Let's	**a**	can have a disco in your garage.
2 You	**b**	buy takeaway pizzas.
3 Why	**c**	have a picnic in the park.
4 Why don't	**d**	can ask your mum to make a cake.
5 We	**e**	don't we go to the cinema?
6 Let's	**f**	we have a party?

b Write the sentences from Exercise 2a below. Then use the words in brackets to write a suitable response.

1 *Let's buy takeaway pizzas.*
(Sorry, / she / not eat / cheese)
Sorry, she doesn't eat cheese.

2 You ....
(OK / mum / loves / make / cakes)
....

3 Why...
(Sorry, / that / boring!)
....

4 Why don't ....
(OK. / We / can / have / it / at my house)
....

5 We ....
(OK. / Meera / love / dancing)
....

6 Let's ....
(That / be / great idea)
....

3 Anna and Meg are out shopping. Complete the dialogues. Use the words in the box.

| can | go | that's | we | ~~why~~ |

Anna: I'm really hot and tired.
Meg: OK. ....*Why*....... don't [1] ....
        have a drink in that café? We
        [2] .... sit outside.
Anna: [3] .... a great idea!
Meg: I think it's raining.
Anna: Yes. Let's [4] .... inside the
        library until it stops.
Meg: Good idea.

4 Anna and Meg are now at home. Complete the dialogue with these words.

| any | don't | haven't | idea | ~~let's~~ |

A: I'm hungry.
B: Me, too. ....*Let's*........ make a Spanish omelette.
A: Good [1] ....
B: OK. Have we got [2] .... eggs?
A: No, we [3] ....
B: Why [4] .... you go to the shop? I can stay here and chop the onions.
A: OK. See you later!

Pronunciation: the /ɪ/ sound

5 🎧 **5.3** **Listen to three sentences. Circle the words that you hear.**

1 **a** this   **b** these
2 **a** living   **b** leaving
3 **a** bin   **b** bean

Writing: describing a picture

6 **Complete the email from Jill with the present continuous form of these verbs.**

dive   have   ~~send~~   sit   sleep   write

7 **Find a photo from a holiday. Answer these questions.**

Where are you?   *on the beach*
What can you see in the photo?
....
What are you doing?
....
Are you on holiday with your family or your friends?
....
What are they doing?
....

8 **Now write an email describing your photo.**

Hi Tom,

I'm on holiday in Florida at the moment. I'm .....*sending*...... you a photo of the hotel. It's fantastic. Can you see the pool? It's really big! It's early in the morning. There's a man in the photo. He ¹............................ into the pool. I ²............................ by the pool. I ³............................ text messages to my friends. You can't see my mum and dad. They ⁴............................ breakfast in the hotel restaurant. You can see my sister. She ⁵............................ on a sunbed.

See you soon,

Jill

Explore more

1 Look at this photo of a group of Inuits inside an igloo. What can you see? Write full sentences with the words below the photo.

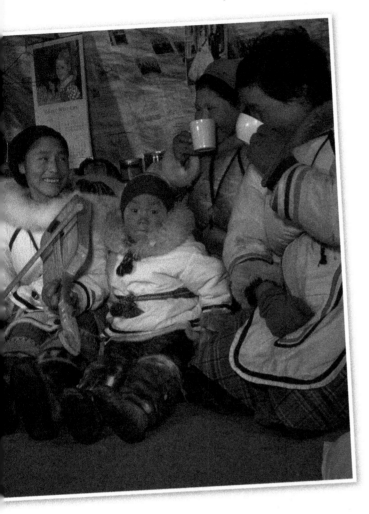

2 Look at this photo and answer the questions. Use full sentences.

1 Where is the man?

....

2 What is he doing?

....

3 What food do you eat outside?

....

3 Look at this photo and answer the questions. Use full sentences.

1 children / sit / floor

....

2 young boy / look / the camera

....

3 women / drink

....

4 newspapers / walls

....

5 girl / smiling

....

2 Look again at the photo of the Inuits and answer the questions. Write full sentences.

1 What are the two women doing?

....

2 What is the girl on the left doing?

....

3 Where do you sit to relax inside an igloo?

....

1 Where are the people?

....

2 What are they doing?

....

3 Where do you usually dance?

....

3 Look at the photo of the girl in her bedroom. Tick (✔) the things you can see.

a bed ☐

books ☐

a chair ☐

a chest of drawers ☐

a desk ☐

shelves ☐

a notebook ☐

a door ☐

a window ☐

4 What is the girl doing? Choose the correct sentence (a, b or c).

a She's lying on the floor.

b She's lying on the bed.

c She's sitting at her desk.

5 Now read the three descriptions. <u>Underline</u> the information that is different to the photo.

a My sister is in her bedroom. There isn't a desk. There isn't a chest of drawers. She's lying on her bed and writing in her notebook.

b My sister is in her bedroom. Her room is big. There's a desk and a chair. She's doing her homework. She's lying on the floor and writing in her notebook.

c My sister is doing her homework in her bedroom. She's sitting at her desk and writing in her notebook. Her books are on the floor.

6 Now choose the correct description (a, b or c) for the photo above.

7 Look at the photo below and choose the correct description (a, b or c).

a In the photo I can see mountains and trees. There's snow on the mountains. There's a river and a tent. A man is sitting by the river.

b There are mountains and snow in the photo. There's a river and some trees. A man is fishing. There's a tent.

c In the photo I can see mountains and a river. There's snow on the mountains and ice on the river. There aren't any trees. A man is looking at the mountains. There's a tent.

Tip! Remember to <u>underline</u> the information that is incorrect!

UNIT 5D EXPLORE MORE **59**

countable and uncountable nouns

Countable nouns are nouns we can count – e.g. *one book* (singular), *two books* (plural). When the subject is plural, the verb is also plural.

This **book** is quite good.   Those **books** are boring.

Uncountable nouns are nouns we can't count (**water, food**, etc). They haven't got a plural form. When the subject is an uncountable noun, the verb is singular.

This **water** is cold.   This **food** is good for you.

1 Complete the table with the words from the list.

book	bread	chair	cheese	food	house
ice	laptop	milk	sandwich	table	water

Countable	Uncountable
book	*food*
1	6 ....
2	7 ....
3	8 ....
4	9 ....
5	10 ....

present continuous (affirmative and negative)

We use **present continuous** to talk about actions that are happening at the moment of speaking, or around this general time.

Brad **is talking** to his father on a webcam.

His parents **are working** in the Antarctic at the moment.

We form the present continuous with **am**, **are** or **is** and the main verb with **-ing**.

I **am** <u>reading</u> a good book at the moment.

You/We/They **are** <u>having</u> lunch now.

He/She/It **is** <u>sitting</u> in the garden.

> With verbs that end in a **consonant + -e**, we change the -e to -ing.
>
> ma**ke**   ma<u>king</u>   ha**ve**   ha<u>ving</u>
>
> With most verbs that end in a **single vowel + a consonant**, we double the consonant and add -ing.
>
> wi**n**   win<u>ning</u>   ge**t**   get<u>ting</u>
>
> With verbs that end in **-ie**, we change the -ie to **-ying**.
>
> lie   l<u>ying</u>   die   d<u>ying</u>

We form the negative by adding the word **not** after **am/are/is**. The short forms are the same as for the verb **be**.

I'm not <u>feeling</u> very well.

You **aren't** <u>listening</u>!

My webcam **isn't** work<u>ing</u> properly.

Affirmative			
I'm You're/We're/ They're He's/She's/It's	(I am) (You/We/They are) (He/She/It is)	studying	for a test now.
Negative			
I'm not (I am not) You/We/They aren't (are not) He/She/It isn't (is not)		studying	for a test now.

2 Complete the sentences with the verbs in the present continuous. Use short forms.

Can you help me? *I'm looking* for my laptop. (**look**)

1 Brad .... a project on climate change at school this week. (**do**)

2 Don't talk on your mobile – you .... a car! (**drive**)

3 We can't play with you now – we .... lunch. (**have**)

4 Anna and Meera aren't here – they .... for clothes. (**shop**)

5 Our cat .... next to me on my bed. (**lie**)

6 I .... my clothes away in my wardrobe. (**put**)

3 Write negative (✗) and affirmative (✔) sentences in the present continuous. Use short forms.

Anna / watch a DVD ✗ / read a book ✔

Anna isn't watching a DVD. She's reading a book.

1 I / do my homework now ✗ / make a sandwich ✔

....

2 Brad and Harry / play basketball ✗ / watch football ✔

....

3 Meera / swim now ✗ / have a rest ✔

....

4 You / sleep ✗ / play computer games ✔

....

5 Bob / practise the piano ✗ / run in the park ✔

....

6 We / lie on the sofa ✗ / sit on the rug ✔

....

present continuous (questions and short answers)

We make questions in the present continuous by putting **Am/Are/Is** before the subject, and then the main verb with **-ing**.

Am _I_ doing this the right way?

Are _you_ listening to music?

Is _it_ raining outside?

In short answers we use **am/'m not, are/aren't** or **is/isn't**. We don't use the main verb.

Questions		
Am Are Is	I you/we/they he/she/it	reading?
Short answers		
Yes,	I am. you/we/they are. he/she/it is.	No,	I'm not. you/we/they aren't. he/she/it isn't.

4 **Write questions in the present continuous. Then write short answers and affirmative sentences.**

Anna / have a bath? No – she / wash her hair

Is Anna having a bath? No, she isn't. She's washing her hair.

You / use the computer? Yes – I / write an email

Are you using the computer? Yes, I am. I'm writing an email.

1 Harry / play football? Yes – he / play in a match

....

2 You / make a cake? No – I / cook a pizza

....

3 Martha and Clark / work in Antarctica? Yes – they/study climate change

....

4 Your mum / shop for clothes? No – she / drive to London

....

5 We / win the match? No – we / play badly

....

there is/are with a, some, any

We use **there is** (singular) and **there are** (plural) to describe what is in a place. In the affirmative, we use **some** with nouns in the plural.

There is _a_ desk in my bedroom.

There are _some_ posters on the walls.

The negative form is **there isn't** (singular) and **there aren't** (plural). In the negative, we use **any** with nouns in the plural.

There isn't _a_ TV in my bedroom.

There aren't _any_ flowers in the room.

We make questions with **Is there** (singular) and **Are there** (plural). In questions, we use **any** with nouns in the plural.

Is there _a_ computer on your desk?

Are there _any_ toys on your bookcase?

Affirmative			
There's There are	a some	book books	on the table.
Negative			
There isn't There aren't	a any	book books	on the table.

Questions			
Is there Are there	a any	book books	on the table?
Short answers			
Yes, there is. Yes, there are.		No, there isn't. No, there aren't.	

5 **Write sentences with there is/are (✔) and there isn't/ aren't (✗). Use a, some and any.**

There is a sofa in the living room. (✔)

There aren't any posters on the wall. (✗)

1 .... magazines on the table. (✔)

2 .... computer in the living room. (✗)

3 .... wardrobe in the bedroom. (✔)

4 .... clothes in the wardrobe. (✔)

5 .... clothes on the bed. (✗)

some and any with uncountable nouns

In **affirmative** sentences, we use **some** before uncountable nouns.

There is **some** _food_ in the kitchen.

We don't use **a** or **an** with uncountable nouns.

In **negative** sentences and **questions**, we use **any** before uncountable nouns.

There is**n't any** _water_ in my glass.

Is there **any** _ice_ in the fridge?

6 **Write questions (?), affirmative (✔) or negative (✗) sentences with these words.**

milk in the fridge (✔) _There is some milk in the fridge_ (✔)

1 paper on my desk (✔)

....

2 bread on the table (✗)

....

3 meat in this food (?)

....

4 plastic in the dishwasher! (✔)

....

6A A school trip

Vocabulary: clothes

1 Find ten more items of clothing in the word square.

X	J	A	C	K	E	T	I	R	D
C	O	A	T	A	Y	S	L	I	C
S	W	E	A	T	S	H	I	R	T
L	H	U	P	N	B	O	O	T	S
P	E	I	W	D	S	E	H	D	J
S	C	A	R	F	E	S	K	R	E
O	A	U	L	T	T	R	S	E	A
O	P	J	W	C	M	S	T	S	N
B	T	R	O	U	S	E	R	S	S
A	F	J	I	L	R	D	E	M	H

2 Complete the descriptions.

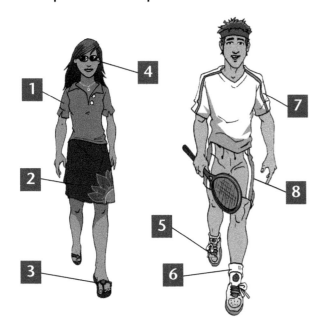

Sandra's wearing a ¹t.op....................... , a
²s.......................... and a pair of ³s.......................... .
She's also wearing ⁴s.......................... .
Jake's wearing a pair of ⁵t.......................... and
⁶s.......................... . He's also wearing a
⁷T-.......................... and ⁸s.......................... .

Vocabulary: places in a town

3 Complete the words.

b a n k

1 c h _ r c h
2 c _ n _ m _
3 m _ s _ _ m
4 p _ r k
5 p _ s t _ f f _ c _

6 r _ s t _ _ r _ n t
7 s h _ p
8 s p _ r t s c _ n t r _
9 s _ p _ r m _ r k _ t

4 Name the places.

You can buy stamps and send letters here.
.....post office..........................

1 You can buy lots of different things here. There are a lot of shelves.

....

2 You can see children playing and people walking.

....

3 There's a big kitchen. You can eat here.

....

4 You can see collections of old things here.

....

5 There's usually a swimming pool and a gym here.

....

Vocabulary: adjectives

5 Complete the sentences with the words in the box.

easy	boring	~~fantastic~~
nice	terrible	

A: I had a ......fantastic.......... time at the party.
B: Yes. It was great!
1 **A:** I love maths.
   B: That's because it's .... for you.
2 **A:** Let's go to the swimming pool.
   B: No thanks. Swimming is ....
3 **A:** Do you like the new Pink CD?
   B: I hate it. It's ....
4 **A:** I like your top. It's really ....
   B: Thanks.

Grammar: *going to*

6 Mrs Jones is going on holiday to Spain with her family. What are her plans? Write sentences with *going to*.

I'm going to relax on the beach.

I / relax / on the beach
I'm going to relax on the beach.

1 we / stay / in a hotel

....

2 I / not / cook

....

3 we / eat / in restaurants

....

4 the children / learn Spanish / in the mornings

....

5 John / go diving / in the afternoons

....

6 we / go to bed late

....

7 Write the sentences in Exercise 6 in the negative form.

I'm not going to relax on the beach.

1 ....

2 ....

3 ....

4 ....

5 ....

6 ....

8 Write questions and short answers about the Jones family.

Mrs Jones / relax / on the beach?

Is Mrs Jones going to relax on the beach? Yes, she is.

1 the family / stay / in a tent?

....

....

2 Mrs Jones / cook?

....

....

3 they / eat / in the hotel?

....

....

4 the children / learn / Spanish?

....

....

5 John / play tennis / in the afternoons?

....

....

6 they / go to bed / early?

....

....

9 Write sentences about your next holiday. Write about yourself and your family. Use the questions below to help you.

- Where are you going?
- Who are you going with?
- When are you going?
- What time are you going to get up / go to bed?
- What are you (not) going to do?

I'm going to France in July with my parents and my sister. We're going by car. My mum and dad are driving.

I'm going to visit my cousins near Marseille.

We're going to go to the beach every morning but we're not going to get up early!

I'm going to go to the sports club with my cousins and I'm going to speak French to their friends!

....

....

....

....

....

....

....

Grammar: *wh-* questions + *going to*

1 Write questions to ask Mrs Jones. Match the questions (1–6) with the answers (a–f).

1 Who / John / go diving with?
Who is John going to go diving with?

2 What clothes / you / take?
....

3 When / the children / play on the beach?
....

4 What / food / they / eat?
....

5 Where / the children / learn Spanish?
....

6 What time / you / go to bed?
....

a At one o'clock in the morning.

b At a language school.

c Shorts and T-shirts, and a dress.

d A diving instructor.

e In the afternoons.

f Paella and fish.

2 Look at the pictures and write two answers. Use these expressions.

> buy a drink   do an exam
> go swimming   order some food
> train in the gym   ~~write a letter~~

1 Why is she sitting at the desk?
  a *Because she's going to write a letter.*
  b ....

2 Why is he going into the sports centre?
  a ....
  b ....

3 Why are they going to go to the restaurant?
  a ....
  b ....

Reading

3 **Look at the photos and tick (✔) the clothes you can see.**

cap	dress	skirt	shirt
sunglasses		top	trousers

4 **Read and match the texts (1–3) with the photos (a–c) in Exercise 3.**

World Fashion

1 Aisha is wearing a beautiful salwar kameez. It's very fashionable in India and in other countries. You can see famous people like Jennifer Lopez and Hillary Clinton wearing the salwar kameez. So, what is it? The salwar is a pair of long, baggy trousers and the kameez is a long shirt. They're very comfortable to wear and very beautiful.

2 Felicia is wearing a long, colourful dress with short sleeves. She's also wearing a scarf on her head, called a head tie. African men wear long, baggy shirts with trousers. African girls like wearing dresses.

3 James is wearing sunglasses and an Australian hat, called an Akubra. Australians like wearing comfortable clothes, like jeans, T-shirts and sweatshirts. In Northern Australia it's very hot, and people wear shorts and sandals. The men even wear shorts to work. The girls sometimes wear dresses.

5 **Read the texts again. Are the sentences true or false?**

	T	F
1 The salwar kameez isn't fashionable in India.	☐	✔
2 An Indian kameez is a long dress.	☐	☐
3 Felicia is wearing a dress with short sleeves.	☐	☐
4 People don't wear jeans in Australia.	☐	☐
5 In Northern Australia, men wear shorts to work.	☐	☐
6 Jennifer Lopez doesn't like wearing the salwar kameez.	☐	☐

Listening

6 🔊 **6.1 Listen to Mike talking to his dad. Circle the correct option to complete each sentence.**

Mike's school is doing a project on *fashion* / *Australia*.

1 The girls think it's going to be *exciting* / *boring*.

2 *Mike's dad* / *Mike* thinks Australians wear cool clothes.

3 Mike is going to look for photos *on the Internet* / *at the library*.

4 At the end of the project, there's going to be *a school trip* / *an exhibition*.

5 Mike is going to wear a *sweatshirt* / *T-shirt* to the party.

6C Shopping

Grammar: possessive 's'

1 Read the texts about world fashion again. Put the apostrophe (') in the correct place.

Aisha's clothes are beautiful.

1 Felicias head tie is beautiful.
2 In Africa, the mens shirts are long.
3 Jamess hat is called an Akubra.
4 In India, the girls trousers are long.

2 Look at the photos from Exercise 3 on page 65. Label these parts of the photos.

James's hat

1 ....

2 ....

3 ....

4 ....

3 What can you see in these pictures? Write sentences.

1 these / the children / toys
These are the children's toys.

2 this / the doctor / bag
....

3 that / my cousin / bike
....

4 these / the boys / dogs
....

5 this / the cat / dinner
....

6 she / the girls / mother
....

Grammar: possessive pronouns

4 Complete the sentences with the possessive pronouns in the box.

~~hers~~ his mine ours theirs yours

The shoes are Maria's. They're ......*hers*...... .

1 The hat is James's. It's ....
2 Our gloves are different. Your gloves are blue. The red gloves are .... !
3 That's my parents' house. It's ....
4 Sam, this isn't my book. Is it .... ?
5 'Are those our bags over there?'
'Yes. They're ....'

Vocabulary: money

5 Write the prices on the price tags.

six euros

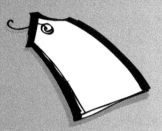

1 five pounds ninety-nine

2 four dollars twenty cents

3 seventy-two pence

4 four euros forty-nine cents

5 twelve pounds fifty

Useful expressions: shopping

6 Complete the dialogue with the expressions in the box.

> Thank you very much.
> And how much are these mugs?
> No, thanks.
> ~~Excuse me.~~
> OK. I'd like the green T-shirt and two mugs, please.
> Here you are.
> How much is this T-shirt?

Mark:	*Excuse me.*
Assistant:	Yes. Can I help you?
Mark:	1..
Assistant:	It's £9.99.
Mark:	2..
Assistant:	They're £4.50 each.
Mark:	3..
Assistant:	Anything else?
Mark:	4..
Assistant:	So, that's £18.99, please.
Mark:	5..
Assistant:	And here's your change.
Mark:	6..

Pronunciation: unstressed sound /ə/

7 a Say the words and circle the unstressed part of the word.

> fashion   August   breakfast   chocolate
> famous   parents   circus   Belgium   island
> sentence   children   ocean

b 6.2 Listen and check.

Writing: write a postcard

8 Imagine you are in one of these countries: India, Kenya or Australia. Think of answers to these questions. Write notes.

a Where are you? *in India ...*

b What is your opinion of the place / the people / the food, etc.?
   fantastic people, great clothes, ...

c What are you doing now?

d What are your plans?

9 Write a postcard to a friend. Use your notes from Exercise 8.

> Dear ....,
>
> I'm in ....
>
> It's ....
>
> At the moment, ...
>
> ....
>
> Tomorrow, ...
>
> ....
>
> See you soon.
>
> Love ....

Reading

1 **You are going to read a text about Kenya. Match these words with the correct headings and complete the table.**

> airport big cats birds bus diving
> elephants fishing flight insects
> jacket plane relax socks
> sunglasses swimming tops

things to do	safari	clothes	travel
....	....	....	....
....	....	....	....
....	....	....	....
....	....	....	....

2 **Read the text and match the sections (1–3) with the photos (a–c).**

1 Kenya is a great country for a holiday. Most holidays in Kenya begin in Nairobi. It's easy to get there by plane. There are international flights to Nairobi airport every day. There is usually a bus waiting at the airport to take you to your holiday destination.

2 Kenya has something for everyone. You can stay in a hotel on the coast and relax on the beautiful beaches. You can do lots of water sports, such as swimming, diving or fishing. You can visit the National Park in Nairobi, or go on an exciting safari where you can see lots of amazing animals and birds.

3 If you go on a safari, it is important to take the right clothes. The sun is very hot and there are lots of insects, so you need long trousers and socks, sunglasses and a hat. It's cold at night, so you also need warm tops or sweatshirts, and a jacket.

3 **Now read the text again and match the sections (1–3) with the headings (a–d). There is one extra heading.**

> **a** What can I do in Kenya?
> **b** When is the best time of year to go on a safari?
> **c** What clothes do I need to take?
> **d** How can I get there?

4 **Which words in Exercise 1 are missing from the text?**

.... and ....

5 a Read the first part of the dialogue in Exercise 6 on page 67. Which word is missing in gap 1?

Mark: Excuse me?
Assistant: Yes. Can I help you?
Mark: How ¹..... is this T-shirt?
Assistant: It's £9.99.

b Choose one of these words (a, b or c) to complete gap 1.

a much   **b** money   **c** price

c Did you choose the correct word to complete the gap?

6 a Read the rest of the dialogue. Which words are missing in the gaps (2–5)?

Mark: And how much are these mugs?
Assistant: They're £4.50 each.
Mark: OK. I'd ².......... the green T-shirt and two mugs, please.
Assistant: Anything ³.......... ?
Mark: No, thanks.
Assistant: So, that's £18.99, please.
Mark: Here you ⁴.......... .
Assistant: And here's your ⁵.......... .
Mark: Thank you very much.

b Choose one of the words (a, b or c) to complete each gap (2–5).

2 a have   **b** take   **c** like
3 a more   **b** else   **c** other
4 a are   **b** have   **c** take
5 a extra   **b** change   **c** coins

c Did you choose the correct words to complete the gaps?

7 Read the dialogue. Complete each gap (1–5) with the correct word (a, b or c).

Assistant: Can I help you?
Ellen: ¹.......... much is this postcard?
Assistant: It's 50p.
Ellen: OK. And how much are ².......... key rings?
Assistant: They're £3 ³.......... .
Ellen: OK. ⁴.......... I have three, please?
Assistant: Of course.
Ellen: And ⁵.......... like four postcards, please.
Assistant: OK. So that's four postcards and three key rings. That's £11, please.

1 a What   **b** How   **c** Is
2 a this   **b** that   **c** these
3 a each   **b** one   **c** all
4 a Am   **b** Do   **c** Can
5 a I'd   **b** I've   **c** I'm

C

Grammar Practice Unit 6

going to

We use **be going to** talk about future plans and to make predictions (what we think will happen).

*I'**m going to** go to the circus this weekend.*

*The sky is blue. It'**s going to** be a nice day.*

We form the **affirmative** with **am/are/is** + **going to** + the bare infinitive of the main verb.

*I'**m going to** stay in London with my sister.*

*We'**re going to** see all the famous sights.*

*My sister'**s going to** take me to Buckingham Palace.*

> Be careful with **be** going (present continuous) and **be** going to go.
>
> *I'**m** going to Meera's house now.* (present continuous)
>
> *I'**m going to** go to Meera's house tomorrow.* (**going to**)

We form the **negative** with **am/are/is** + **not** + **going to** + the bare infinitive of the main verb.

*I'**m not going to** do your homework for you!*

*Brad and Harry **aren't going to** play basketball this evening.*

*I'm sure it **isn't going to** rain tomorrow.*

Affirmative			
I'm You're/We're/They're He's/She's/It's	(I am) (You/We/They are) (He/She/It is)	going to	have a party.
Negative			
I'm not (I am not) You/We/They aren't (are not) He/She/It isn't (is not)		going to	have a party.

We make questions by putting **am/are/is** before the subject, and then **going to** + the bare infinitive of the main verb.

Am I going to win the race?

Are they going to visit their grandparents?

Is Meera going to come to the party?

In short answers we use **am/'m not, are/aren't** or **is/isn't**. We don't use the main verb.

*Are you going to meet your friends? – Yes, I **am**.*

*Is Brad going to go to Paris? – No, he **isn't**.*

Questions				
Am Are Is	I you/we/they he/she/it	going to	make	breakfast?
Short answers				
Yes,	I you/we/they he/she/it	am. are. is.	No,	I'm not. you/we/they aren't. he/she/it isn't.

1 Write sentences with *going to*. Use short forms.

I / go / to the cinema tomorrow

I'm going to go to the cinema tomorrow.

1 Harry / go / to bed early tonight

....

2 you / be / late for school!

....

3 we / play / basketball after lunch

....

4 Brad's dad / call / him tonight

....

5 Anna and Meera / have / a great time in Paris

....

2 Write negative sentences with *going to*. Use short forms.

I / not / eat / any chocolate today

I'm not going to eat any chocolate today.

1 Bella / not / go / to the disco with Ron

....

2 we / not / wear / our uniforms on the school trip

....

3 your team / not / win / the match tomorrow

....

4 I / not / buy / lots of souvenirs on holiday

....

5 it / not / rain / today

....

3 Write questions with *going to*.

we / have / pizza for dinner, Mum?

Are we going to have pizza for dinner, Mum?

1 your dad / drive / you to the airport?

....

2 David / go / diving on holiday?

....

3 Anna and Meera / climb / to the top of the Eiffel Tower?

....

4 Brad / visit / his parents in Antarctica?

....

5 Anna / need / lots of clothes in Paris?

....

4 Now write affirmative (✔) or negative (✗) short answers to the questions in Exercise 3.

(Are we going to have pizza for dinner, Mum?)
(✔) *Yes, we are.*

1 ✔ ....

2 ✗ ....

3 ✔ ....

4 ✗ ....

5 ✔ ....

5 Write questions with *going to*.

What presents / Anna / buy?
What presents is Anna going to buy?

1 Where / they / go shopping?

....

2 What time / Tariq / phone us?

....

3 When / you / do / your homework?

....

4 What / we / cook / for dinner?

....

5 Who / Josh / visit / tomorrow?

....

possessive s'

We use **possessive s'** to show who or what something belongs to.

Where is the dog's food bowl? (It belongs to the dog.)

We use **'s** after a person's name, even if it ends in **s**.

This is Anna's book. (It belongs to Anna.)

Do you like Charles's shoes? (They belong to Charles.)

We use **'s** after a singular noun.

That is my friend's house. (One friend lives there.)

When the noun is plural, the apostrophe (') goes after the **s**.

That is my friends' house. (Two or more of my friends live there.)

> **BUT** when the noun has an irregular plural, we use **'s**.
>
> *This is the children's room.* (It belongs to two or more children.)
>
> *Young people's hairstyles are strange.* (the hairstyles of young people)

6 Write the underlined words with an apostrophe.

That's Meeras T-shirt. *Meera's*

1 I think both my parents clothes are boring. ....

2 Where are these girls new shoes? ....

3 This year's childrens fashions are really exciting.

....

4 Why are you wearing your mums skirt? ....

5 Tesss hair looks great! ....

7 Write sentences with possessive apostrophes.

they / that boy / books. *They're that boy's books.*

it / those dogs / food. *It's those dogs' food.*

1 they / those girls / shoes

....

2 it / those people / car

....

3 it / that woman / purse

....

4 they / that man / children

....

5 they / those policemen / uniforms

....

possessive pronouns

A **possessive pronoun** replaces a **possessive adjective + noun**. The possessive pronoun is the same for singular and plural nouns.

These are my shoes. (possessive adjective + noun)

*They are **mine**.* (possessive pronoun)

*Do you like my hairstyle or **hers**? – I like **yours**.*

*Is this his shirt? – Yes, it's **his**.*

*Those aren't their bags – they're **ours**. **Theirs** are over there.*

Possessive adjectives							
my	your	his	her	its	our	you	their
Possessive pronouns							
mine	yours	his	hers	its	ours	yours	theirs

8 Complete the sentences with possessive pronouns.

Those look like Meera's trainers. I'm sure they're ......*hers*......

1 That isn't Brad's suitcase. .... is blue.

2 You've got your jackets with you but we haven't got ....

3 That isn't their uniform. .... is grey and white.

4 I often borrow Meera's clothes, and she borrows ....

5 Harry, we've got exactly the same jeans! Mine are just like .... !

1 Write sentences and questions using the present continuous.

1 Mike/a sandwich/eat.

....

2 talk/Bill and Karen/on the telephone?

....

3 in the sea/Suzie/swim.

....

4 you/listen/to the radio?

....

5 do/their homework/they.

....

1 mark per item: ... / 5 marks

2 Complete the sentences using *There is/Is there* or *There are/Are there.*

1 .... a sandwich on the table.
2 .... some plates in the dishwasher.
3 .... any CDs on the shelves?
4 .... a recycling bin in the kitchen?
5 .... some bags in the drawer.

1 mark per item: ... / 5 marks

3 Choose the correct words.

1 I have **any/some** cheese in the kitchen.
2 There aren't **any/some** towels in the bathroom.
3 There is **any/some** food in the cupboard.
4 Is there **a/any** table in your bedroom?
5 There are **any/some** bananas in the bowl.

1 mark per item: ... / 5 marks

4 Complete the sentences using five of these words or phrases.

| any | is melting | is standing | is taking |
| some | are | isn't | |

1 I've got .... paper in the study.
2 The ice .... in Antarctica.
3 There .... two rooms in the cabin.
4 Is there .... pasta in the cupboard?
5 Joe .... a shower at the moment.

2 marks per item: ... / 10 marks

5 Write sentences with *going to.*

1 go sailing/I/next week

....

2 they/around the world/travel

....

3 Paul/the museum/visit/tomorrow

....

4 write/on her blog/she

....

5 we/our money/spend/on clothes

....

1 mark per item: ... / 5 marks

6 Add an apostrophe where necessary.

1 Both boys have short hair.

....

2 Angelas shoes are black and shiny.

....

3 The childrens trousers are comfortable.

....

4 The blue baseball cap is Garys.

....

5 Both girls skirts are long and grey.

....

1 mark per item: ... / 5 marks

7 Complete the sentences with possessive pronouns.

1 That's my suitcase. It's ....
2 That's my cousins' computer. It's ....
3 This is your money. It's ....
4 This is my family's car. It's ....
5 That's Amy's purse. It's ....

1 mark per item: ... / 5 marks

8 Complete the sentences and questions with *going to.*

1 .... your black boots? (you/wear)
2 .... some fancy dress clothes for the party. (she/buy)
3 .... to the cinema this weekend? (we/go)
4 .... those croissants? (they/not eat)
5 .... German on my holiday in Berlin. (I/speak)

2 marks per item: ... / 10 marks

9 Complete the sentences using these words.

> bins   dishwasher   fridge
> cabins   shower

1 Have you got a ...... in your bathroom?
2 The scientists live in warm ....
3 We put our rubbish into ....
4 The dirty plates go in the ....
5 Can you put the milk back in the ...... ?

1 mark per item: ... / 5 marks

10 Match the activities to the places.

1 read a text message   **a** in the park
2 watch a DVD   **b** on a mobile phone
3 go for a walk   **c** on TV
4 go swimming   **d** in the kitchen
5 cook dinner   **e** at the beach

1 mark per item: ... / 5 marks

11 Choose the correct words.

1 She always **recycles/rebuilds** plastic bottles.
2 This camera uses **rechargeable/remade** batteries.
3 He **posts/sends** emails to his friends.
4 **Close/Switch** off the lights, please.
5 We want to **stay/save** water.

1 mark per item: ... / 5 marks

12 Complete the sentences using five of these words.

> bed   doors   drawers   rug
> shelves   table   wardrobe

1 I keep my books on those ....
2 Is this the ...... you sleep in?
3 You can hang your clothes in that ....
4 I keep my t-shirts in a chest of ....
5 I've got a ...... on the floor to keep it warm.

2 marks per item: ... / 10 marks

13 Match the words to their opposites.

1 easy ...   **a** long
2 great ...   **b** difficult
3 exciting ... **c** tired
4 energetic ... **d** terrible
5 short ...   **e** boring

1 mark per item: ... / 5 marks

14 Complete the sentences using these words.

> cap   jackets   skirts
> sunglasses   trainers

1 Boys don't wear ....
2 She wears a baseball ...... on her head.
3 I wear dark ...... to protect my eyes.
4 She is wearing ...... for running.
5 They are wearing ...... on top of their t-shirts.

1 mark per item: ... / 5 marks

15 Complete the sentences using these words.

> calendar   magnet   key ring
> postcard   stamps

1 You can buy ...... at the post office.
2 This fridge ...... is a nice colour.
3 His ...... makes a noise in his pocket.
4 Circle your birthday on the ....
5 We are going to send you a ...... when we are on holiday.

1 mark per item: ... / 5 marks

16 Complete the sentences using five of these words.

> designing   going   organising   rising
> sailing   staying   wearing

1 Sea levels are ....
2 My sisters are ...... a fancy dress party.
3 We are ...... on holiday soon.
4 He is ...... a website for the company.
5 The boat is ...... across the lake.

2 marks per item: ... / 10 marks

Total: ... / 100

7A Celebrations

Vocabulary: adjectives

1 Circle the correct adjective.

Toby is (ill) / bored.

1 Lily is *bored / happy.*

2 James is *nervous / ill.*

3 Natalie is *excited / nervous.*

4 Jenni is *scared / excited.*

5 Ralph is *tired / hungry.*

6 George is *ill / hungry.*

Vocabulary: irregular verbs

2 Match the sentence beginnings (1–6) and endings (a–f).

Last week was Josh's birthday.

1 He gave
2 His sister bought
3 His sister said
4 His mum made
5 Josh saw
6 His friends read

a a cake.
b the invitation.
c his friends at school.
d his friends an invitation to his birthday party.
e 'Happy Birthday'.
f a present.

3 Circle the correct verb to continue the story about Josh's birthday party.

The party (began) / went / made at seven o'clock.

1 His friends *came / had / began* to the party.

2 His brother *ate / drank / made* fruit juice.

3 They *gave / bought / ate* some cake.

4 His mum *made / had / took* some photos.

5 His friends *had / went / made* home at half past nine.

4 Complete Josh's email with these words.

~~had~~	had	gave	wrote	won

On Saturday, I ....*had*......... a birthday party. I ¹........................... a great time. My friends ²........................... me presents and my brother ³........................... every game. On Sunday, I ⁴........................... thank-you letters.

Grammar: past simple *be*

5 Complete the sentences with *was* or *were*.

Josh ...*was*... fourteen last week.

1 It .... Josh's party on Saturday.

2 The party .... at his house.

3 His friends .... at the party.

4 I .... there too.

5 There .... a chocolate birthday cake.

6 We .... all very happy.

6 Write questions and short answers. Use the information from Exercise 5.

............*Was*............ Josh fourteen last week?

...*Yes, he was.*...

1 .... Josh's party on Saturday?
....

2 .... the party at a restaurant?
....

3 .... his friends at the party?
....

4 .... you there too?
....

5 .... there a chocolate birthday cake?
....

6 .... everyone happy?
....

7 Write questions.

When / you / born *When were you born*?

1 Where / you / born
.... ?

2 Who / your / first teacher
.... ?

3 What / your / favourite toys
.... ?

4 Who / your / best friend at primary school
.... ?

Past time expressions

8 Complete the expressions with these words.

~~at~~ last ago yesterday in last

...............*at*............... six o'clock.

1 two years ....

2 2007

3 .... night

4 .... week

5 .... evening

Grammar: past simple regular verbs (affirmative)

9 Add *-d* or *-ed* to form the past tense of these regular verbs.

arrive..*d*........   celebrate......*d*......   change..............
cook..............   divorce..............   enter...............
finish..............   form..............   invite..............
join..............   listen..............   live..............
look..............   open..............   play..............
record..............   start..............   work..............

Tip! Be careful! Some regular verbs have changes to the past tense.
study – studied
travel – travelled

10 Write sentences. Use the words in the boxes. Use the past simple form of the verbs.

arrive ~~celebrate~~ live	at for in ~~last~~
open play start	on yesterday

I ...*celebrated*...... my birthday ...*last*... week.

1 We .... football .... Sunday.

2 The bus .... late .... morning.

3 My parents .... in Canada .... six years.

4 The new gym .... 2007.

5 The film .... seven o'clock.

11 Write six true sentences with the words.

I	watch	TV	last week
My friends	play	the dinner	at the weekend
Our class	cook	to music	last night
My father	listen	hard	yesterday
My mother	work	basketball	on Sunday
Our teacher	arrive	late	this morning

Our class played basketball last week.

....

....

....

....

....

....

Reading

1 Read the text and match the paragraphs (1–4) with the pictures (a–d).

When I was a kid

1 When Steven Spielberg was six years old, his father took him and his three sisters to a big field near their house. It was midnight. There, they watched meteors crossing the dark sky. Spielberg included this experience in his film *Close Encounters of the Third Kind*. In the film, a father wakes his children to watch lights from a *spaceship*.

2 Steven watched a lot of TV when he was a kid. "A lot on TV scared me," says Steven. "And so did other things – like my sisters' toy clown, the trees outside my bedroom window and my dark wardrobe." Later, he put all of those things in his film *Poltergeist*. "As a kid, I liked being scared," says Steven. "It helped my imagination."

3 When he was twelve, Steven wanted to make films. He made films with his father's camera. His family and friends were the 'film stars'. He also practised *special effects*. With his mother's help, he cooked a red fruit dessert until it exploded. There was red fruit all over the kitchen. Then he filmed it.

4 Steven filmed at the weekends, and on Mondays he didn't want to go to school. He liked to stay at home to *edit* his films. Sometimes he said he was ill. He put a thermometer next to the ceiling light and his mum believed him. This is exactly what Elliot did in the film *E.T.*

2 Read the text again. <u>Underline</u> the titles of three Steven Spielberg films.

3 Read the text again. Are the sentences true or false?

	T	F
When Steven was three, his father took him to a field.	☐	✗
1 Steven and his sisters saw meteors in the sky.	☐	☐
2 When he was a boy, Steven was never scared.	☐	☐
3 Steven's mum helped him do special effects.	☐	☐
4 Steven made films at school.	☐	☐
5 He was often ill on Mondays.	☐	☐

Steven put the thermometer next to the ceiling light.

The family watched meteors in the night sky.

Steven practised special effects in the kitchen.

Steven was scared of many things.

Listening

4 🔘 *7.1–7.2* **You are going to listen to two dialogues. Match them with the pictures (a–b).**

a

Our wedding
Dialogue ....

b

Our summer holiday
Dialogue ....

7 🔘 *7.2* **Listen again and correct the false sentences in Exercise 6.**

....
....
....
....

Grammar: past simple irregular verbs (affirmative)

8 **Complete the table with the infinitive or the past simple form of the verbs.**

Irregular verbs	
Infinitive	**Past simple**
begin	....
....	bought
....	came
drink	....
eat	....
....	gave
go	....
have	....
....	made
....	read
say	....
see	....
take	....
....	won
....	wrote

5 🔘 *7.1* **Listen again to David and Hannah (Dialogue 1). Match the questions (1–6) with the answers (a–f).**

1 Who looked beautiful?   **a** David
2 Who was worried before the wedding?   **b** Hannah's brother
3 Who arrived late?   **c** David's mother
4 Who was nervous?   **d** David's father
5 Who danced all night?   **e** Hannah
6 Who talked all night?   **f** Hannah

6 🔘 *7.2* **Listen again to Meg and Anna (Dialogue 2). Are the sentences true or false?**

	T	F
Meg and Anna went on holiday to France last year.	☐	☒
1 They went with Anna's family.	☐	☐
2 Anna wore pink sunglasses.	☐	☐
3 The girls hated camping.	☐	☐
4 It was Meg's eleventh birthday.	☐	☐
5 Anna's parents took them to a restaurant to celebrate.	☐	☐
6 They bought Meg a present.	☐	☐

9 **Complete the text. Use the past simple form of these verbs.**

| ~~be~~ | be | come | eat | give | go |
| read | say | take | write | | |

I can remember my first day at school. I ....*was*.......... four years old. My mum
[1]........................... me to the school in the morning. I [2]........................... sad when she [3]........................... goodbye. In the morning, we [4]........................... our names on our books. Then the teacher [5]........................... us some milk. At lunchtime, we [6]........................... our sandwiches. In the afternoon, the teacher [7]........................... a story. My mum [8]........................... to the school at 3.15 and we [9]........................... home.

Vocabulary

1 Complete the dialogues. Write *Congratulations!*, *Happy Birthday!* or *Good luck!*

   A: It's my birthday today.
   B: *Happy Birthday!* ....

1 **A:** Our daughter was born last night.
   B: ....

2 **A:** It's our wedding anniversary next week.
   B: ....

3 **A:** We are going to live in America.
   B: ....

4 **A:** I passed my driving test last week!
   B: ....

2 **a** Put the parts of the dialogue in order.

Meg:	OK. Where's the party?	☐
Meg:	Thanks, I'd love to!	☐
Meg's mum:	Oh, hello, Anna. Just a moment.	☐
Anna:	Well, it's my grandparents' wedding anniversary next week. We're going to have a big celebration next Saturday. Would you like to come?	☐
Meg's mum:	Yes, who is it, please?	☐
Anna:	It's at the Grand Hotel. It starts at one o'clock.	☐
Anna:	Hi, can I speak to Meg, please?	1
Meg:	Hi, Anna, what's up?	☐
Meg:	OK, see you on Saturday! Bye!	☐
Anna:	Bye!	☐
Anna:	It's Anna.	☐
Anna:	Great. There's going to be a meal and then dancing. Your parents can come too.	☐

b 🔊 7.3 Now listen and check.

Useful expressions: invitations

3 Complete the responses.

   A: Can I speak to Mark, please?
   B: Of ....*course*........ . Just a moment.

1 **A:** Can you come to my party?
   B: Thanks, ... love to.

2 **A:** It's my birthday today.
   B: .... Birthday!

3 **A:** I'm going to have a baby.
   B: .... !

4 **A:** Would you like to come to the cinema?
   B: I'm .... , I can't.

5 **A:** We're having a barbecue. Can you come?
   B: .... is it?

Pronunciation *-ed* endings

4 🔊 7.4 Listen to the verbs and write them in the table.

~~arrived~~   ~~celebrated~~   changed   climbed   ~~cooked~~   finished   helped   invited   lived   looked   opened   packed   started   travelled   worked

1 /t/	**2** /d/	**3** /ɪd/
cooked	arrived	celebrated
....	....	....
....	....	....
....	....	
....	....	

Writing: an invitation and a reply

5 Look at this invitation to Anna's grandparents' wedding anniversary. Complete the invitation and the reply. Use the words in the box.

at	at	for	having	hope
~~it's~~	on	to	with	

Dear Carol and Steve,

.....It's..... Jack and Mary's

50th Wedding Anniversary

¹.............. Sunday, 8 June.

We're ².............. a celebration dinner

³.............. the Grand Hotel ⁴..............

one o'clock. We ⁵.............. you can come.

Bill and Alice

Dear Bill and Alice,

Thank you ⁶.............. your invitation to Jack and Mary's anniversary dinner.

We'd love ⁷.............. come and celebrate ⁸.............. you.

Best wishes,
Carol and Steve.

6 a Write an invitation to a special occasion.

b Now write a reply to the invitation.

Listening

1 Now do these exercises.

1 *7.5* Listen to an answerphone message. Write the missing information (1–4) in the following note. You can listen to the message twice.

> **Message**
> For: [1] ....
> From: [2] ....
> Message: Cinema this
> [3] .... ?
> Meet outside the [4] ....
> at three o'clock.

2 *7.6* Listen to an answerphone message. Write the missing information (5–8) in the following note. You can listen to the message twice.

> **Message**
> For: [5] ....
> From: [6] ....
> Message: Shopping tomorrow
> Catch the bus at [7] ....
> o'clock.
> [8] .... her tonight.

3 *7.7* Listen to an answerphone message. Write the missing information (9–12) in the following note. You can listen to the message twice.

> **Message**
> For: [9] ....
> From: Your sister, Sally
> Message: [10] It's .... on Sunday.
> Dinner at [11] .... at 1.30.
> Take some [12] .... !

4 *7.8* Listen to an answerphone message. Write the missing information (13–16) in the following note. You can listen to the message twice.

> **Message**
> For: [13] ....
> From: Julie
> Message: They're going to come to the
> [14] .... on [15] ....
> See you at the [16] ....

5 *7.9* Listen to an answerphone message. Write the missing information (17–20) in the following note. You can listen to the message twice.

> **Message**
> For: Steve
> From: [17] ....
> Message: Surprise party for Penny
> It's on [18] .... She's leaving for
> [19] .... next week.
> Can you bring
> [20] .... ?

2 **Match the celebrations (1–6) with the pictures (a–f).**

1 a birthday party
2 a wedding anniversary
3 a wedding
4 Mother's Day
5 a christening
6 a New Year's Eve party

3 **Match the statements (1–3) with the responses (a–c).**

1 Can I speak to Darren, please?   **a** Yes. I'd love to.
2 Can you come to my party?   **b** Happy Birthday!
3 It's my birthday!   **c** Of course. Just a moment.

4 **Now do these questions.**

1 **7.10** Listen to six short statements twice. Choose the best response (a, b or c).

> **Tip!** Before you listen, think of a statement (or question) for each response.

1 a Thanks, I'd love to.
  b See you there.
  c Happy Birthday!
2 a What's up?
  b OK. What time?
  c Who is it, please?
3 a I'm sorry, I can't.
  b OK. When?
  c Who is it, please?

4 a What's up?
  b See you there.
  c Of course. What time?
5 a Good luck!
  b Congratulations!
  c What's up?
6 a Congratulations!
  b See you there.
  c I'm sorry, I can't.

2 **7.11** Listen to six short statements twice. Choose the best response (a, b or c).

1 a Thanks, I'd love to.
  b Yes, of course.
  c OK. What time?
2 a What's up?
  b OK. What time?
  c Congratulations!
3 a OK. When?
  b Good luck!
  c See you there!
4 a What's up?
  b I'm sorry, I can't.
  c See you there!
5 a OK. What time?
  b Who is it, please?
  c What's up?
6 a Who is it, please?
  b OK. When?
  c I'm sorry, I can't.

3 **7.12** Listen to six short statements twice. Choose the best response (a, b or c).

1 a Hi. What's up?
  b Who is it, please?
  c Of course. Just a moment.
2 a Yes, of course.
  b Good luck!
  c Congratulations!
3 a Of course. Just a moment.
  b Thanks. I'd love to.
  c What's up?
4 a Congratulations!
  b Good luck!
  c OK. When?
5 a Happy Birthday!
  b Congratulations!
  c I'm sorry, I can't.
6 a OK. What time?
  b OK. See you there!
  c Thanks. I'd love to.

Grammar Practice Unit 7

past simple be

The **past simple** of the verb **be** is **was** and **were**.

I was in Spain last month.

*He/She **was** very nervous at the wedding.*

*It **was** hot and sunny yesterday.*

*You/We/They **were** very tired last night.*

The negative is **was not** (**wasn't**) or **were not** (**weren't**).

*I **wasn't** happy about what happened yesterday.*

*He/She **wasn't** at school two days ago.*

*You/We/They **weren't** hungry at lunchtime.*

Affirmative		
I	was	
You/We/They	were	at home yesterday evening.
He/She/It	was	

Negative		
I	wasn't (was not)	
You/We/They	weren't (were not)	at school last Sunday.
He/She/It	wasn't (was not)	

We make questions by putting **was** or **were** before the subject.

Was *I fat when I was a baby?*

Were *you/we/they late for school on Monday morning?*

Was *he/she excited about going on holiday?*

Was *it a good book?*

Questions		
Was	I	
Were	you/we/they	asleep at 1.00 a.m. last night?
Was	he/she/it	

Short answers						
	I	was.		I	wasn't.
Yes,	you/we/they	were.	No,	you/we/they	weren't.
	he/she/it	was.		he/she/it	wasn't.

Time expressions we use with past simple:

• in 1991/2005/etc

• **yesterday**

• **last night**

• **last Tuesday/week/month/winter/year/etc**

• two/etc **hours/days/weeks**/etc **ago**

These expressions can go at the beginning or at the end of a sentence.

*I was at home **last night**.*

Last month *Mum and Dad were on holiday.*

---

1 Complete the sentences with *was/were* (✔) or *wasn't/weren't* (✗).

It ....*was*.............. my parents' wedding anniversary last Tuesday.

1 He .... hungry at lunchtime. (✗)

2 I .... in Italy on holiday last summer. (✔)

3 The players .... nervous before the big match. (✔)

4 You .... late for school yesterday. (✗)

5 Anna .... at Meera's birthday party last Saturday. (✔)

6 We .... friends at primary school. (✔)

2 Write questions from these sentences.

Anna's party was at First Light disco.
........*Was Anna's party at First Light disco?*........

1 It was Anna's tenth birthday.
....

2 All of Anna's friends were there.
....

3 Anna was very excited.
....

4 I was the first guest to arrive.
....

5 It was a fantastic party.
....

6 We were very bored.
....

3 Now write affirmative (✔) or negative (✗) short answers to the questions in Exercise 2.

(Was Anna's party at First Light disco?) (✔)
.................*Yes, it was.*.................

1 (✗) ....
2 (✔) ....
3 (✔) ....
4 (✗) ....
5 (✔) ....
6 (✗) ....

4 Put the words in the correct order to make questions.

your favourite subject/was/what/last year?
...*What was your favourite subject last year?*...

1 who/with/you/were/yesterday afternoon?
....

2 unhappy/was/why/Jill/at lunchtime?
....

3 they/were/where/on Tuesday?

....

4 how long/were/in France/we/last year?

....

5 swimming training/what time/was/yesterday?

....

5 Choose the correct words to complete the time expressions.

Where was Brad ......*yesterday*...... afternoon? (**last/yesterday**)

1 Who was Anna with .... night? (**last/yesterday**)

2 Were you here .... lunchtime? (**at/on**)

3 We were at the party .... four hours. (**ago/for**)

4 This disco wasn't here two years .... (**ago/before**)

5 Were you born .... 1997? (**on/in**)

past simple regular verbs (affirmative)

We form the past simple of regular verbs by adding **-ed** to the verb. This is the same for all subjects.

I/He/She <u>wanted</u> a new computer.

We/They <u>remembered</u> to send her a birthday card.

> With verbs that end in **-e**, we add **-d**.
> lik**e**   like<u>d</u>   us**e**   us<u>ed</u>
> With verbs that end in a **vowel + -y**, we add **-ed**.
> sta**y**   stay<u>ed</u>   pla**y**   play<u>ed</u>
> With verbs that end in a **consonant + -y**, we change the **-y** to **-ied**.
> tr**y**   tr<u>ied</u>   hurr**y**   hurr<u>ied</u>
> With most verbs that end in a **single vowel + consonant**, we double the consonant and add **-ed**.
> fi**t**   fit<u>ted</u>   trav**el**   travel<u>led</u>

> There are some irregular verbs in English. We do NOT form the past simple of these verbs by adding **-ed**.
> For example:
> Present: **be   come   do   get   go   have   make**
> Past: **was   came   did   got   went   had   made**

We use the past simple to talk about:

• actions, events or situations which started and finished in the past.

*We **lived** in Spain for two years.*

• habits in the past.

*My parents **travelled** a lot when they were young.*

• actions in the past which happened one after the other.

*He **washed** his face, **brushed** his teeth and **walked** down the stairs.*

6 Complete the sentences with the past simple form of the verbs.

Anna ....*looked*........ beautiful in her party clothes. (**look**)

1 I .... to make a cake yesterday, but it was a disaster! (**try**)

2 We .... in London at half past nine. (**arrive**)

3 Brad .... to watch an English football game. (**want**)

4 Anna and Meera .... for clothes all day yesterday. (**shop**)

5 Mum .... the piano when she was a child. (**play**)

7 Complete the table with the missing forms.

Infinitive	Past simple
be	was
begin	began
1	bought
2 come	....
3 do	....
4	got
5	gave
6 go	....
7	had
8 make	....
9	put
10	said
11 take	....
12	wrote

8 Complete the sentences with the past simple form of the verbs.

I ....*bought*........ her a DVD as a birthday present. (**buy**)

1 Brad .... a project on climate change at school last week. (**do**)

2 Anna and Meera .... to Paris on a school trip. (**go**)

3 We .... lunch about an hour ago. (**have**)

4 This morning I .... an email to my friend in New Delhi. (**write**)

5 Mum .... pizza for dinner last night. (**make**)

6 I .... my clothes away in my wardrobe yesterday. (**put**)

8A Back in the USA

Vocabulary: technology

1 **Complete the words.**

1 p r i n t e r
2 s c r _ _ n
3 s p _ _ k _ r s
4 w _ b c _ m
5 m _ m _ r y s t _ c k
6 k _ y b _ _ r d
7 m _ _ s _

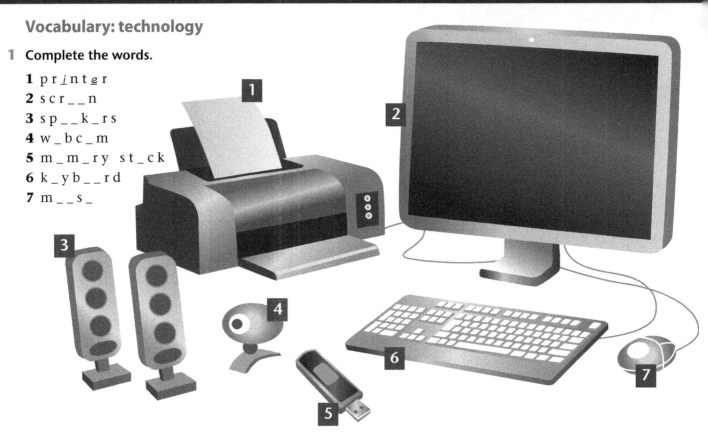

2 **Use the words in the screen to complete the gaps below.**

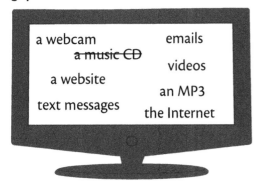

a webcam   emails
a music CD
                            videos
a website
                            an MP3
text messages
                            the Internet

1 two things you can listen to: ....*a music CD*....
  and ....

2 something you can watch: ....

3 two things that you write and send, or receive
  and read: .... and ....

4 something that you look at: ....

5 something you use to see people:
  ....

6 something you go on: ....

Vocabulary: irregular verbs

3 **Complete the story with these words.**

~~bought~~	found	left	lost	put	sent
sold	spoke	stuck	thought	went on	

On Saturday, Carol went to a shop. She
....*bought*....... a new memory stick. At the library,
she [1]........................ the Internet. She [2]........................
a good website. The website [3]........................ books
and CDs online. She [4]........................ the web
address on her memory stick and [5]........................
some emails. Then she [6]........................ the Internet
connection.

At home, Carol looked for her memory stick
but it wasn't in her bag. 'Oh no!' she
[7]........................ . 'I [8]........................ it at the library
this morning!' She phoned the library and
[9]........................ to the library assistant. The
assistant said, 'Don't worry. I've got it.' Carol
[10]........................ a note on the fridge for her mum
and went back to the library.

Vocabulary: adverbs

4 Choose the correct word.

He's copying the CD
(badly) / well.

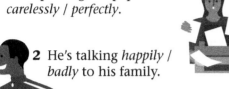

1 She's putting the paper in
carelessly / perfectly.

2 He's talking *happily /
badly* to his family.

3 She's playing music
loudly / quietly.

4 She's typing
slowly /quickly.

5 She's watching a DVD
loudly / quietly.

6 He's typing *quickly / slowly.*

Grammar: past simple (questions and short answers)

5 Read the text in exercise 3 on page 84 again. Write questions and short answers with *did*. Don't forget to use prepositions.

Carol / buy / a book?

Did Carol buy a book?
No, she didn't.

1 she / go / the library?

....

....

2 the website / sell / clothes?

....

....

3 she / write / the web address / her notebook?

....

....

4 she / lose / the connection?

....

....

5 she / put / the memory stick / her bag?

....

....

6 Write questions about Carol with these words.

What / Carol / buy?
What did Carol buy?

1 Where / she / go next?

....

2 Why / she / go / there?

....

3 Where / she / leave / memory stick?

....

4 Who / she / speak to?

....

5 What / she / stick / the fridge?

....

7 Now answer the questions in Exercise 6.

She bought a new memory stick.

1 ....

2 ....

3 ....

4 ....

5 ....

8 a Complete the quiz questions. Use *What, Which, Where, When* or *Who* and the correct form of the verb.

1 ....*What did*.......... Percy Lebaron Spencer
..........*design*........ ? (design)

2 .... university ....
Einstein .... to? (go)

3 .... Marie Curie ....
from? (come)

4 .... Robert Cailliau
.... with? (work)

5 .... John Logie Baird
.... in 1925? (invent)

6 .... Neil Armstrong
.... on the moon? (walk)

b Match the questions (1–6) with the answers (a–f).

1–f

a In 1969.
b Sir Timothy Berners-Lee.
c Swiss Federal Polytechnic School, Zurich.
d Television.
e Warsaw, Poland.
f The microwave oven.

Inventions

Reading

1 Match these words with the pictures (1–4).

~~crown~~ gold weigh scales

1 c.*r o w n*........

2 s..................

3 w..................

4 g..................

2 Read the text. Match the pictures (a–b) with two of the paragraphs.

Archimedes and the golden crown

1 Archimedes was a famous scientist and inventor. He was born in 287 BC in Syracuse. This was a Greek city in Sicily but he went to school in Egypt. There are many stories about Archimedes. One famous story is about Archimedes and the golden crown.

2 The king had a new gold crown. But he didn't believe it was all gold. He said to Archimedes, 'I think the men who made my crown put *silver* in it. I think they stole some of the gold.' The king asked Archimedes to discover if this was true.

3 One day Archimedes was in the bath. He thought about what happens when you put gold and silver in water. Then he understood what to do! He jumped out of the bath and ran down the street with no clothes on, shouting 'Eureka!' (I found it!)

4 So what did Archimedes do? He took the crown and some gold. The gold weighed the same as the crown. He put them onto some scales. Then, he carefully put them into a big sink of water. The scales didn't balance in the water and so Archimedes discovered that the crown wasn't all gold.

3 Read the text again. Choose the correct answer (a, b or c).

Where was Archimedes born?

a in Egypt

b in Greece

c in Sicily

1 What did the king ask Archimedes to do?

a make a new crown

b help him with a problem

c find the people who stole his gold

2 Where was Archimedes when he shouted 'Eureka!'?

a in the bath

b in the street

c on the beach

3 Where did Archimedes put the crown?

a in the bath

b on his head

c in a sink

4 What did Archimedes discover?

a there wasn't any gold in the crown

b there was silver and gold in the crown

c there was only gold in the crown

Grammar: past simple (negative)

4 a Read this sentence from the text.

But he didn't believe it was all gold.

b Find one more sentence in the text with *didn't*.

....

5 Complete the sentences with the negative past simple form of these verbs.

| eat | hear | ~~sleep~~ |
| study | understand | win |

Tina is very tired. She ....*didn't sleep*.... well last night.

1 Max only got four marks in his test. He .... before the exam.

2 Ben is very hungry. He .... any lunch.

3 The team played badly. They .... the match.

4 The maths homework was very difficult. I .... it.

5 John was late for school. He .... his alarm clock.

Listening

6 **Read and listen to the first part of a dialogue. Choose the best picture (a or b).**

Mark: Hi, Sandra. What are you doing?
Sandra: I'm looking at this magazine about the solar system. It's really interesting.
Mark: I saw a solar eclipse once, in 1999.
Sandra: What's a solar eclipse?
Mark: It's when the moon covers the sun.
Sandra: What happened?
Mark: Well, I was about five years old. I was with my family in France. In the morning we bought some special glasses. But somebody stole mine! I left them on a table in the café and when I went back they weren't there!
Sandra: What did you do?
Mark: My dad gave me his.

7 Answer the questions.

When did Mark see the eclipse?
  He saw it in 1999.

1 Where was he?
....

2 Who did he go with?
....

8 Read the second part of the dialogue. Choose the best picture (c or d).

Sandra: So, what about the eclipse?
Mark: Well. The moon started to cover the sun, and it went very quiet and windy. Then it began to get dark.
Sandra: Did it go completely dark?
Mark: No, it didn't. There was a yellow circle of light round the moon. I took my glasses off and my mum shouted at me. I think she was scared.
Sandra: Why was she scared?
Mark: Because you can hurt your eyes if you look at an eclipse, even if you look at it quickly or accidentally.
Sandra: Oh. So, when is the next eclipse?
Mark: I don't know. Isn't it in your magazine?

9 Answer the questions.

1 Where did Mark leave his glasses?
....

2 Why did Mark's mum shout at him?
....

3 What can happen if you look at an eclipse?
....
....

1 Complete the text with these words.

~~Earth~~	planets	solar	stars
sun	sun	telescope	universe

Copernicus didn't believe that the ....*Earth*.......... was the centre of the 1.. . He believed that the 2.. was the centre of the 3.. system. He said the Earth and the 4.. went round the 5.. .

Galileo Galilei looked at the 6.. with his 7.. and wrote about Copernicus's ideas.

2 Complete the text about Albert Einstein's early life with these words. There is one extra word.

carefully	carelessly	clearly	hard	perfectly

Albert Einstein was born in Ulm, Germany on 14 March, 1879.

He was very clever and worked 1.. at primary school. When he was six, he built mechanical models, which worked 2.. !

When he was ten, a family friend gave him books to read about mathematics and science. Einstein thought 3.. about the things he read and began to do his own mathematical investigations.

When he was a teenager, he didn't enjoy secondary school and didn't pass his exams. He left at sixteen. That year, he performed his first famous thought experiment. In the experiment, he was travelling along a beam of light. He saw this 4.. in his imagination.

3 Choose the most logical adverb.

Many inventions happen (accidentally) / carelessly.

1 Archimedes put the crown *carefully / perfectly* into the water.

2 Mark remembered the eclipse *carefully / clearly*.

3 The Earth moves *carelessly / slowly* round the sun.

4 Scientists work *accidentally / hard* to make new discoveries.

5 Radio signals cook food *clearly / perfectly*.

Pronunciation: the /ɔː/ sound

4 a Say the words.

sport	bored	thought	born
talk	call	bought	four
saw	walk	form	more

b ⊙ 8.2 Now listen and check.

Useful expressions: telling a story

5 Complete the sentences about the dialogue in exercise 8 on page 87. Use *then, first* and *when*.

1 .... it went very quiet.

2 .... the moon started to cover the sun, it began to get dark.

3 .... the eclipse happened slowly.

6 Now complete these sentences about Einstein. Use *then, first, when* and *but*.

1 Einstein was a very clever child. .... he made his own models, and .... he did mathematical investigations.

2 .... Einstein was 16, he performed his first thought experiment.

3 He was a good student at primary school .... he didn't like secondary school.

Writing: a story

7 **Complete Jill's sentences. Match the beginnings (1–7) with the endings (a–g).**

1 Last week, I played ——
2 I didn't have a nice sweatshirt, so
3 We played the match
4 I went home. I discovered that
5 I ran quickly back to the sports centre
6 I phoned the coach. She said,
7 She came to the sports centre

a but the sweatshirt wasn't there!
b 'Don't worry. I saw it and put it in my bag.'
c I borrowed my sister's.
d in a volleyball championship.
e and we won.
f and gave it to me.
g I didn't have the sweatshirt.

8 **Write notes to answer these questions about the story in Exercise 7.**

When did it happen? *last week*

Where did it happen? *at the volleyball match*

1 What did Jill forget/lose? ....

2 What did she do? ....

3 What did she do then? ....

4 What did Jill's coach tell her? ....

5 What did Jill's coach do? ....

9 **Now write out the story. Add *when, first, then* and *but* in a suitable place.**

Last week Jill played in a volleyball championship. She didn't have a nice sweatshirt, so ....
....
....
....
....
....
....
....
....
....
....
....
....

10 **Think of a time when you lost something or when you forgot something. Write notes to answer the questions. Put the verbs in the past tense.**

1 Where were you? ....
....

2 Who were you with? ....
....

3 What did you forget/lose? ....
....

4 What did you do? ....
....

5 What happened then? ....
....
....

11 **Write the story in your notebook. Remember to add words like *when, first, then* and *but*.**

....
....
....
....
....
....
....
....
....
....
....
....
....
....
....
....
....
....

Reading

1 **Read this summary of the dialogue in Exercise 8 on page 87. Choose the correct answer (a, b or c).**

> Mark: We were on holiday in France. On the day of the eclipse we wore special glasses. When the moon started to cover the sun, it began to get dark. First, it went very quiet and it began to get windy. The eclipse happened very slowly. There was a yellow circle of light round the moon. When I took my glasses off, my mum shouted at me. You can hurt your eyes if you look at an eclipse, even if you look at it quickly or accidentally.

The summary is about

a Mark's holiday in France.

b the day of the eclipse.

c Mark's accident.

2 **Now do these exercises.**

1 Read the text. Choose the correct answer (a, b or c).

> People ate ice cream back in Roman times. The Roman emperor Nero (A.D. 37–68) told his men to bring ice from the mountains and mix it with fruit. King Tang (A.D. 618–97) of China created mixtures of ice and milk. Europeans brought ice cream to Europe from China. Ice cream arrived in the United States in 1700. The first ice cream shop opened in New York City in 1776. Americans were the first to use the word 'ice cream'.

The text is about

a different types of ice cream.

b the history of ice cream.

c American ice cream.

2 Read the text. Choose the correct answer (a, b or c).

> In 2001, students from Holland invented Nuna, a new solar-powered car. It competed in the 2001 World Solar Challenge, a 3,000 km race across Australia. Nuna finished first and broke four world records. It won the race again in 2003. The Dutch students used Kevlar to make the car. This is a material used in satellites. The car is covered with solar cells that work when there's no sunlight. These were also developed for satellites.

The text is about

a satellites.

b Australian motor-racing.

c a solar-powered car.

3 Read the text. What is the text about? Choose the correct answer (a, b or c).

> In 2005, scientists discovered a new animal in the rain forests of Borneo (in south-east Asia), but they don't know what exactly it is. The animal is about the size of a house cat and has red fur. It walked in front of a night-time camera put there by World Wildlife Fund researchers. The camera caught only two images, which were not very clear. The scientists showed the photos of the animal to Bornean wildlife experts. Most experts believe it is a new species of carnivore. Scientists hope to catch a live animal one day.

The text is about

a cats in Borneo.

b scientific cameras.

c a mysterious animal.

3 Look again at the dialogue about the eclipse in Exercises 6 and 8 on page 87. Match the questions (1–5) with the answers (a–f). There is one extra answer.

1 When did it happen?
2 Who was Mark with?
3 Where did it happen?
4 What did Mark do?
5 What did his mum do?

a He left his glasses in the café.
b In 1999.
c He stole some glasses.
d In France.
e He was with his parents.
f She shouted at him.

4 Now do these exercises.

1 Match the questions (1–4) with the answers (a–e). There is one extra answer.

1 Where did you go?
2 When did you go?
3 Who did you go with?
4 Where did you stay?

a I went with the school.
b In a hotel.
c I went to Vienna.
d I visited the old city.
e I went two weeks ago.

Study tip!
Match the easy ones first.

2 Match the questions (1–4) with the answers (a–e). There is one extra answer.

1 What happened?
2 Where were you?
3 What did you do?
4 Did they find it?

a No, I didn't.
b I told the police.
c I lost my bag.
d No, they didn't.
e I was on the train.

3 Match the questions (1–4) with the answers (a–e). There is one extra answer.

1 Where did you go?
2 What did you see?
3 Was it good?
4 Who did you go with?

a Yes, it was great.
b I went with my sister.
c We saw a French film.
d I saw my teacher.
e To the cinema.

4 Match the questions (1–4) with the answers (a–e). There is one extra answer.

1 Did you do your homework?
2 Where is it?
3 Why did you put it there?
4 What happened?

a It's in the bin.
b Yes, I did.
c I dropped it in the street.
d It was very difficult.
e Because the paper was dirty.

Grammar Practice Unit 8

past simple (questions and short answers)

We make questions in the past simple by putting **Did** before the subject, and then the bare infinitive of the main verb. This is the same for regular and irregular verbs, and the same for all subjects.

Did I/we/he <u>tell</u> you about my new computer?
Did you <u>miss</u> your dog while you were away?
Did he/she/they <u>go</u> to Scotland?

In short answers, we use **did** or **didn't**. We <u>don't</u> use the main verb.
*Did Brad like England? – Yes, he **did**.*
*Did his parents visit him? – No, they **didn't**.*

Questions				
Did	I/you/we/they/he/she/it		send	an email?
Short answers				
Yes,	I/you/we/they/he/she/it	did.	No, I/you/we/they/he/she/it	didn't.

We can use **question words** to ask for information. We begin with the question word, followed by **did**.
What <u>did</u> Meera buy? – A pair of trainers.
When <u>did</u> he start learning Spanish? – Two years ago.
What time <u>did</u> the train arrive? – At 4 o'clock.
Where <u>did</u> you find my keys? – In the bathroom.
Why <u>did</u> she go to the city centre? – To buy new clothes.
How <u>did</u> you get to school this morning? – I walked.

1 Write questions from these sentences.

Brad liked living in England.
Did Brad like living in England?

1 Christopher Columbus discovered America.

....

2 Football practice started an hour ago.

....

3 Brad and Harry played basketball yesterday.

....

4 Brad missed his dog when he was in England.

....

5 The dog stayed in the USA.

....

6 Brad loved eating Indian food.

....

2 Put the words in the correct order to make questions.

you/speak to/did/your teacher/yesterday?
Did you speak to your teacher yesterday?

1 invent/Alexander Graham Bell/did/the telephone?

....

2 Anna and Meera/go/to Paris/did/on a school trip?

....

3 a good time/you/did/have/on holiday?

....

4 Brad/did/any/eat/French food?

....

5 live/your best friends/do/in your street?

....

3 Write affirmative sentences in the past simple. Use prepositions where necessary.

Brad/take/lots of things/England
Brad took lots of things to England.

1 Anna/buy/souvenirs/Paris

....

2 Brad/go/Paris/with Anna and Meera

....

3 Brad/speak/his friends/the computer

....

4 Brad/try/cook/fish and chips

....

5 He/see/his parents/the webcam/every week

....

4 Now write affirmative (✔) or negative (✘) short answers to the questions in Exercise 3.

Did Brad take lots of things to England?
(✘) No, he didn't.

1 ....
  (✔) ....
2 ....
  (✘) ....
3 ....
  (✔) ....
4 ....
  (✘) ....
5 ....
  (✔) ....

5 Put the words in the correct order to make questions.

Brad/when/did/go/to England?

When did Brad go to England?

1 where/he/did/live?

....

2 he/did/who/stay with?

....

3 did/where/Brad's parents/go?

....

4 they/did/go/why/there?

....

5 how long/stay/Brad/did/in England?

....

6 did/he/which English food/love?

....

6 Write questions for these answers.

What time did the train leave?

The train left <u>at 4.05 p.m</u>.

1 ....?

We bought <u>a new printer</u>.

2 ....?

Elena found Jack's keys <u>under the sofa</u>.

3 ....?

Harry got to school <u>at half past nine</u>.

4 ....?

I woke up at ten o'clock <u>because I didn't hear my alarm clock</u>.

5 ....?

Kezia went to the party with <u>Jeremy</u>.

adverbs of manner (regular and irregular)

Adjectives describe nouns, and adverbs describe verbs – that is, they say how someone does something. We form most adverbs by adding *-ly* to the adjective.

He is a <u>careful</u> driver. He drives <u>carefully</u>.

It's a <u>quiet</u> printer. It prints <u>quietly</u>.

It's a <u>slow</u> computer. It works <u>slowly</u>.

> There are some irregular adverbs that don't end in *-ly*:
>
> **well hard fast early late high low straight**
>
> *They are <u>good</u> dancers. They dance **well**.*
>
> *You're a <u>hard</u> worker. You work **hard**.*
>
> *She's a <u>fast</u> runner. She runs **fast**.*

7 Read these short paragraphs. Tick (✔) the words that are correct and correct the mistakes.

He was a **careful** ......✔........ worker and he did his job ~~good~~ ....*well*.... He always worked (1) **hard** .... and he was a (2) **quickly** .... thinker. He arrived at work (3) **early** .... every day and left (4) **lately** ....

We called the ambulance and it arrived (5) **quickly** .... , but not (6) **quiet** .... The "dee-dah" siren was (7) **loudly** .... as it drove very (8) **fast** .... along the road.

past simple (negative)

The **negative** of the past simple is *did not* and the bare infinitive of the main verb. This is the same for regular and irregular verbs, and the same for all subjects. The short form is *didn't*.

*You/She/They **didn't** <u>invite</u> me to the party.*

*I/We **didn't** <u>hear</u> the phone ringing.*

*He **didn't** <u>think</u> his invention was important.*

Negative			
I/You/We/They He/She/It	didn't (did not)	know	the answer.

8 Match the beginnings (1–5) with the endings (a-e). Then write sentences in the negative past simple.

1 ~~he/not/know the answer~~ because

2 he/not wake up

3 the printer/not/work

4 he/not/phone the school

5 he/not/answer the phone

a he/not/hear it ringing

b he/not/switch it on

c ~~he/not/understand the question~~

d he not hear his alarm clock

e he/not/remember the number

He didn't know the answer because he didn't understand the question.

1 ....

2 ....

3 ....

4 ....

Review Units 7 and 8

1 Complete the sentences with the past simple form of be.

1 Paul .... excited about the wedding.

2 My cousins .... happy at the party.

3 The burger and chips .... delicious.

4 She .... very fashionable when she was young.

5 They .... bored in the museum.

1 mark per item: ... / 5 marks

2 Complete the sentences with the past simple form of the verbs.

1 They .... sightseeing in London. (enjoy)

2 We .... in France for two years. (live)

3 She .... television last night. (watch)

4 He .... the piano last weekend. (practise)

5 I .... my grandparents on Monday. (telephone)

1 mark per item: ... / 5 marks

3 Complete the sentences with the correct preposition.

1 The baby was born .... Friday.

2 The party is going to be .... April.

3 We ate dinner at six o'clock.

4 Our wedding is .... 24th July.

5 My grandmother lived .... a small house.

1 mark per item: ... / 5 marks

4 Complete the sentences with the past simple form of the verbs.

1 Our dad .... us a bedtime story. (read)

2 My friend .... me a delicious salad. (make)

3 The party .... at 9 p.m. on Saturday. (begin)

4 She .... she was nervous about the exam. (say)

5 My teacher .... me lots of homework. (give)

2 marks per item: ... / 10 marks

5 Complete the sentences with the past simple form of the verbs.

1 My big brother .... my birthday party. (prepare)

2 We .... the football game last night. (not/watch)

3 I .... to heat the food in the microwave oven. (forget)

4 Christopher Columbus .... India. (not/discover)

5 Christine .... her new mobile phone to school. (not/take)

1 mark per item: ... / 5 marks

6 Complete the past simple questions.

1 .... to the cinema two days ago? (she/go)

2 .... a nice cake for your birthday? (they/make)

3 .... you a text message about the party? (she/send)

4 .... on time? (they/arrive)

5 .... to France last summer? (David/travel)

1 mark per item: ... / 5 marks

7 Choose the correct words.

1 **Where/Who** did he stay with?

2 **When/Where** did they travel to Australia?

3 **Who/Why** did she go to Paris?

4 **What/When** did they see in New York?

5 **When/Which** cities did you visit?

1 mark per item: ... / 5 marks

8 Complete the sentences.

ago	last	forgot	found	were

1 My parents .... born in the 1970s.

2 We went to Ireland on holiday .... summer.

3 I .... your phone number. I just can't remember it.

4 Yesterday, I .... the money you lost in my room.

5 My grandparents visited Greece twenty years ....

2 marks per item: ... / 10 marks

9 **Complete the sentences with these words.**

| excited hungry ill |
| nervous tired |

1 We are .... We are going to eat lunch now.

2 I was .... about going on holiday. I love the beach.

3 Sam was .... about the flight. He is scared of flying.

4 Nadia is very .... We are taking her to see the doctor.

5 He wanted to sleep because he was ....

1 mark per item: … / 5 marks

10 **Complete the sentences with these words.**

| drank gave saw |
| took wrote |

1 My sister .... a famous actor at the shopping centre.

2 We .... our dog to see the vet yesterday.

3 Ryan .... a glass of orange juice at breakfast.

4 My dad .... a letter yesterday.

5 She .... me a present on my birthday.

1 mark per item: … / 5 marks

11 **Write the past simple form of the verbs.**

1 eat ....

2 buy ....

3 go ....

4 make ....

5 see ....

1 mark per item: … / 5 marks

12 **Complete the sentences with the past simple form of the verbs.**

| begin come form |
| record win |

1 She .... a pop group with her friends.

2 The lesson .... at ten o'clock.

3 They .... their first CD ten years ago.

4 He .... a prize for his painting.

5 They .... to my house last week.

2 marks per item: … / 10 marks

13 **Complete the sentences with these words.**

| email Internet MP3 |
| text message website |

1 We can listen to an .... on my computer.

2 He is writing a .... on his mobile phone.

3 Last night, I looked at a .... about my favourite band.

4 I'm going to send you an .... at the weekend.

5 My brother uses the .... to play games and shop online.

1 mark per item: … / 5 marks

14 **Choose the correct words.**

1 Did you go **at/to** the shops yesterday?

2 Did Jane arrive **in/on** June?

3 Which city do you live **at/in**?

4 Who did you stay **on/with**?

5 Did they stay at home **at/on** Monday?

1 mark per item: … / 5 marks

15 **Choose the correct words/**

1 We were late for school, so we ran **perfectly/ quickly**.

2 Marie is from France. She speaks French **perfectly/badly**.

3 They won the game because they played **loudly/well**.

4 I didn't hear him because he spoke **quickly/ quietly**.

5 Her old computer worked **carelessly/badly**, so she bought a new one.

1 mark per item: … / 5 marks

16 **Complete the sentences with five of these adverbs.**

| accidentally carefully hard |
| happily clearly slowly |

1 They were tired, so they walked .... to the house.

2 Bob smiled .... when he won the prize.

3 Lynne wanted to send me an email, but she .... sent it to her brother.

4 John always works .... He is never lazy.

5 The children were scared of falling down. They skated .... on the ice.

2 marks per item: … / 10 marks

Total: … / 100

Reading Explorer

Reading Explorer

The Reading Explorer section of this book helps you with your reading skills. There are interesting things to read on different topics, with wonderful illustrations. The reading passages come with fantastic photographs maps, charts and graphs which give lots of information.

Reading skills

When you look at a text, try to decide what kind of text it is by looking through it quickly. For example, a newspaper article tells you the general idea of the text, the *gist,* in the headline and the opening lines of the first paragraph. Other articles give you an introduction to a problem and then build on a topic over several paragraphs, with a concluding paragraph that sums up the whole thing.

Knowing where to look for the information you need in different kinds of texts is a very important skill and it saves time.

Reading for *gist*, or *skimming*

This is the name for what you do when you quickly look through a text to get the general idea, the *gist*, of what it is about.

Reading for particular information, or *scanning*

This is when you look through a text to find some particular facts or information.

These skills help you read quickly, and the Reading Explorer activities help you to develop both of them.

Vocabulary

It's very important to remember that you don't need to understand every word in order to understand the meaning of the whole text. On the other hand, reading texts gives you the chance to learn many new words.

You can't always read a text with a dictionary next to you, so it's important to learn the skill of deciding the meaning of an unknown word from its context. This is called *inference.*

- First, look at the position of the unknown word in the sentence. For example, adjectives always come before the noun they are describing in English; this will help you to see what the word is doing in the phrase.
- Next, look and see if it has any familiar parts to give you a clue.
- Then look at the other words around it and see how they are connected to the unknown word.

By building up these skills, you will become an independent reader.

It is a good idea to have a special notebook, or a file, where you keep a list of new words. You can write the word by itself, with a translation of its meaning in your own language. Also write one or two examples of how it is used – a phrase or sentence with the word in it. It is difficult to remember a new word when you only see it once, so go back and revise the new words regularly.

Enjoy your reading!

Reading Explorer

Unit 1: Around the world   page 98

Unit 2: Amazing animals!   page 100

Unit 3: What's for dinner?   page 102

Unit 4: Climbing the walls   page 104

Unit 5: Penguins – true or false?   page 106

Unit 6: The new seven wonders of the world   page 108

Unit 7: Amazing kids   page 110

Unit 8: Cool inventions   page 112

Around the world

1 Read the texts. Match the texts (1–4) with the photos (a–d).

Ayers Rock, Australia

The Coast Mountains, Canada

1 This country is very big. It's very cold in winter. It's north of the *equator* – when it's winter here, it's summer in Australia. *Grizzly bears* and *polar bears* are from this country. The capital is Ottawa and the money is dollars. Its languages are English and French.

2 This country is very big. It's very hot in summer but it isn't very cold in winter. This country is south of the *equator* – when it's autumn here, it's spring in England. *Koala bears* and *kangaroos* are from this country. The capital is Canberra and the money is dollars. The language is English.

3 This country has got two big islands. They're called the South Island and the North Island. They're in the Pacific Ocean, south of Australia. It's not very hot in summer and it's cold in winter. The capital is Wellington. It's on the North Island. *Kiwi birds* and *kiwi fruit* come from this country. The money here is dollars and the languages are English and Maori.

4 This country is an island. It's in north-west Europe. It's cold in winter and it's very *wet*. It's very green. It's a country with lots of *sheep* and birds. Grey *seals* are from this country too. The capital is Dublin and the money is Euros. Its languages are English and Irish.

Galway, Ireland

Fiordland National Park, New Zealand

2 Find one photo from Australia, one from Ireland, one from New Zealand and one from Canada.

a

This is an Inuit boy. He lives near the Arctic.

b

This is the Great Barrier Reef. It's a coral reef and it's very long.

c

This is a building in Dublin. It's on the river Liffey.

d

This man is a Maori warrior. He's in the forest. He's from the North Island.

Amazing animals!

Find out about these amazing animals.
Match the texts (1–4) with the photos (a–d).

a *Polar bear cub*

b *Chameleon*

1 **A big cat**

This animal is from Africa and southern Asia. It can run up to 96 kilometres an hour. It is seven times *stronger* than humans and can carry two to three times its own weight. It can *climb* trees.

2 **Tired?** *Thirsty?* **No, not me!**

This animal is from Africa and the Middle East. It has got one big *hump*. It is called the *ship of the desert* and can go for several months without water. It can drink almost 100 litres of water in ten minutes. It can carry more than 225 kilograms for 64 kilometres. It has only got two toes on each foot. Its hump stores *fat* for *energy* when it does not have water.

c Leopard

3 *Fast food*

This is a type of *lizard* that has got a long, *sticky tongue* that can *shoot out* of its mouth at 21.5 kilometres per second to catch a *bug*! It can also move each eye in a different direction and its special *tail* means it is good at climbing trees. Its *speciality* is colour. It can change from green to brown, blue, yellow, red, black, white or a *mixture* of each depending on its *surroundings* or its *mood*!

4 A good *swimmer*

These bears live in Russia, Norway, Greenland (Denmark), Alaska (USA) and Canada. The *males* weigh 550 kilograms and the *females* only 300 kilograms. They can swim almost 100 kilometres without a rest. They can run at 40 kilometres per hour and jump over 6 feet in the air. They have *amazing appetites* and can eat ten per cent of their *body weight* in less then an hour. They are very *patient* and can sit for days at a *seal hole* without moving.

d Dromedary camel

What's for dinner?

Read about these unusual foods. Which ones would you eat?

Yum yum! Witchetty grubs!

Witchetty Soup!

Is it possible? *Grubs* for dinner?! In Australia people eat Witchetty Soup. It's a soup with grubs in it. The grubs are called 'witchetty grubs'.

And people all over the world eat lots of different insects.

In Bali, people eat *dragonflies* with rice. In Africa, they eat *ants*, and in Indonesia children love *roasted stinkbugs*.

Fried dragonflies served with rice.

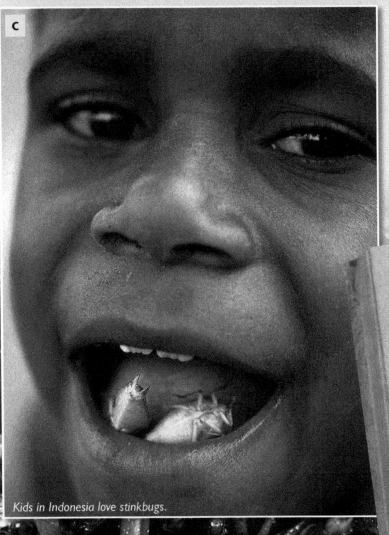

Kids in Indonesia love stinkbugs.

Do you like cooking? Try this recipe for chocolate chip and mealworm cookies!

1 Mix eggs, *flour* and butter in a bowl.

2 Add the chocolate chips.

3 Add the meal worms.

4 Put spoonfuls of cookie mix on a tray.

5 Bake in the oven for 10 minutes at 200°C.

Clockwise from top left : **1** *a bowl of baby bees* **2** *grasshoppers* **3** *larvae* **4** *pupae*

In Japan, restaurants serve a selection of bugs on a plate. They are a very special dish.

Bugs are healthy. They are in the same food group as chicken and fish.

Caterpillars are a very healthy food too. Eat 20 caterpillars a day and you have got all the *calcium* and *iron* you need for healthy bones and teeth.

Mmmmmmmmm!
Chocolate crickets!

So, what's for dessert?

In restaurants in Australia you can order *'Honey Ant Dreaming'*. This dessert has an ant on top of cream and chocolate. Yum, yum!

Or, how about apple with *worms*?!

Ants!

Climbing the walls

What do you think? Read the text and answer the questions.

1 Is indoor climbing safe or dangerous?
2 Can you climb on your own?
3 Do you need to wear a helmet?

Where do climbers go climbing? They usually climb mountains but these climbers are different.

Brent Hill, 15, climbs a wall at the Upper Limits Rock Gym. The wall is 20 metres high and Brent is tired. "Come on!" says his friend, Josh, 14. "You're almost there!" Brent moves his hand to the next *handhold*. He moves his feet to the next *ledge*. He finally gets to the top.

The Upper Limits Rock Gym is inside old silos. Silos are enormous *cylinders*. You can see them on farms.

There are different *routes*. Indoors, the climbers can climb to the top of the silos. Outdoors, they can climb the old *elevator*.

Lindsey Reu, 14, climbs a wall and Brent Hill belays.

The Upper Limits Rock Gym is inside this old building.

This is the old elevator.

These cylinders are the old silos.

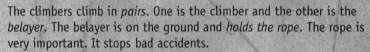

The climbers climb in *pairs*. One is the climber and the other is the *belayer*. The belayer is on the ground and *holds the rope*. The rope is very important. It stops bad accidents.

Indoor climbing is *safe*. The climbers practise difficult moves with Chris Schmidt. He's the climbing instructor. "You don't need a *helmet* indoors because rocks can't fall on your head," says Chris. "But you need good climbing shoes."

Matthew Malmgren, 15, Andre Walker, 12, and Josh, practise their knots.

It's great fun too. "When you get to the top, you're very tired," says Josh. "But you also feel really good. It's fantastic!"

Match the clues with the sports.

BMX racing

Sailing

Baseball

1 You play in a team. You play with a *bat* and a ball.

2 You race in competitions. You wear a *helmet*.

3 You perform in competitions. You move fast and wear fantastic *costumes*.

4 You do this on water. You need a *boat* and a *life-jacket*. You can *race* in competitions.

5 You do this in the sea. You use a *board*. You *ride the waves*.

Ice-skating

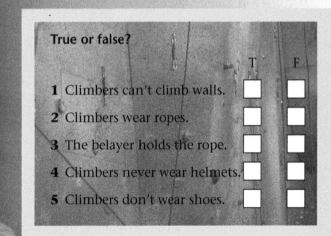

Surfing

Climbing Quiz

True or false?

	T	F
1 Climbers can't climb walls.	☐	☐
2 Climbers wear ropes.	☐	☐
3 The belayer holds the rope.	☐	☐
4 Climbers never wear helmets.	☐	☐
5 Climbers don't wear shoes.	☐	☐

Penguins – true or false?

Happy Feet is a film about Mumble. He's a young *emperor penguin* and he's got blue eyes. Read about Mumble and real penguins and do the True/False quiz.

a

Penguins have got blue eyes

Look at this photo of a real emperor penguin *chick*.

In real life, emperor penguins have got black eyes.

	T	F		T	F
In the film:	☐	☐	In real life:	☐	☐

b

Penguins can sing

In the film, the emperor penguins can sing. Mumble is different. He can't sing but he can dance.

Look at this photo of an emperor penguin.

This penguin is calling to its chick.

Emperor penguins *call loudly*. Each penguin has got a special call. They call to *attract a mate* and to call to their chicks. They don't really sing.

	T	F		T	F
In the film:	☐	☐	In real life:	☐	☐

c

Penguins can dance

In the film, Mumble arrives on the coast of South America. He meets five *Adélie penguins*. These penguins love mambo dancing and they make friends with Mumble.

Look at this photo of an Adélie penguin.

In the photo a *male* Adélie is 'dancing'. He's moving his *flippers up and down* and he's moving his head *from side to side*. Male Adélies dance to attract a mate.

	T	F		T	F
In the film:	☐	☐	In real life:	☐	☐

A male Adélie dances to attract a mate.

d Penguins can jump

In one *scene* in the film, Mumble is swimming under the ice. A hungry *leopard seal* swims after him. Mumble jumps out of the water onto the ice, where he is *safe*.

A leopard seal is a great swimmer.

In this photo, a leopard seal is swimming in the cold water. Leopard seals *kill* and eat penguins. They are great swimmers but they can't move well on the ice.

Penguins move well on the ice.

In this photo, a penguin is jumping out of the water onto some ice. Penguins can swim, jump and move well on the ice.

	T	F		T	F
In the film:			**In real life:**		

e Penguins steal stones

The Adélie penguins in the film like collecting *stones*. They also take stones from other penguins.

Look at these photos:

An Adélie penguin is sitting on its nest.

Adélies make their *nests* with stones. And they *steal* stones from other penguins when they are sleeping!

An Adélie with a stone in its beak.

In this photo, an Adélie penguin is carrying a stone in its *beak*. Now, where is that stone from?

	T	F		T	F
In the film:			**In real life:**		

The new seven wonders of the world

You're going on a trip around the world. You are going to visit the new seven *wonders* of the world.

Which of the countries below do you think you are going to visit?

USA
BRAZIL
ITALY
CHINA
JORDAN
MEXICO
EGYPT
INDIA
PERU

Read about the new seven wonders of the world and say which country they are in.

a

The Great Wall is 6,400 kilometres long. It goes over mountains, through rivers and across deserts. It is about 4.6 metres wide and it has got thousands of *towers*, *castles* and *temples* along it. You can walk along the wall and you can see it from the moon.

Country: ....

b

Machu Picchu is an ancient city built by the Incas. It is over 600 years old. A lot of the buildings in the city are *ruins*. It is built on the top of a mountain, 2,400 metres *above sea level*. Machu Picchu has three main buildings. These are the 'Intihuatana', the 'Temple of the Sun', and the 'Room of the Three Windows'.

Country: ....

Christ the Redeemer is a *statue* of Jesus Christ in Rio de Janeiro. The statue is 38 metres tall. It is built of *concrete* and stands on top of the Corcovado mountain. This mountain is 700 metres high. The statue looks over the city and it is the tallest statue like this in the world.

Country: ....

c

The Colosseum is an *amphitheatre* in the centre of the city of Rome. Today, many parts of the Colosseum are ruins but it is an important example of Roman *architecture*. It is very popular and many tourists visit it. You can see the Colosseum on the country's five-cent euro coin.

Country: ....

Chichen Itza is an *ancient* Mayan city in the north of the Yucatán *peninsula*. The city has got lots of enormous *stone* buildings. There are pyramids and many temples. In the centre of Chichen Itza is a *square* pyramid called the 'Temple of Kukulkan' (the castle). It has steps on all four sides and you can climb to the temple at the top.

Country: ....

The Taj Mahal is a very famous white building. It is in the city of Agra. It has an enormous white *dome* and four tall *towers*. It is built *in memory of* the *Emperor* Shah Jahan's favourite wife. The Taj Mahal is an example of 'Mughal' architecture. This means it has styles from India and from Persia.

Country: ....

Petra is an ancient city in the *valley* of 'Wadi Araba'. The city is built of pink rock from the mountains. There are many *ruins* in Petra. The most amazing ruin is called 'Al Khazneh'. There is also an enormous *amphitheatre*. This amphitheatre has got mountain walls on three sides.

Country: ....

Answer: a China, **b** Peru, **c** Brazil, **d** Italy, **e** India, **f** Mexico, **g** Jordan

Amazing kids

Then ...

Read about these *child prodigies*. Match the texts (1–3) with the photos (a–c).

a

b

c

1 Patrick Bossert
Twickenham, England

In 1982 when he was thirteen years old, Patrick Bossert wrote a book called *You can do the cube*. His book explained how to *solve* the Rubik's Cube. He then wrote a book for children called *Micro-games*. This book explained how to write computer games. He also *developed* online games with his friends. When Patrick was twenty-one years old, he *set up* a computer *software company*. In 1999, he *invented* the 'Delta-T Probe' which finds *bugs* in computer systems. He had a new idea almost every day. "I love finding *solutions* to difficult problems," he said.

2 Michelle Kwan
California, USA

Michelle Kwan started skating when she was five years old. Her older sister, Karen, was also a skater. When Michelle was eight years old, they woke up at 3 a.m. and trained for three hours before school. When she was thirteen, she was a young skating star. When she was twenty, she won her third world championship and she won a silver medal at the Olympics. She also studied arts at the University of California. "College is great but so is skating," she said in 2000. "I want a life with many *sides*, not just skating."

3 Sergio Salvatore
New Jersey, USA

When he was four years old, Sergio started piano lessons with his dad. When he was thirteen, he played jazz piano in concerts in Japan, Italy and Canada. He also *composed* music for two albums and performed on one of the albums with the famous jazz pianist Chick Corea. When he was nineteen, he was at university studying computer science, but he also practised the piano three to four hours a day. "I hope to *combine* these interests one day," he said. "But music comes first."

...and now

Quiz

Who said ... ?

a "I want a life with many sides, not just skating."

b "I love finding solutions to difficult problems."

c "I hope to combine these interests one day. But music comes first."

Are they doing these things (a–c) today?

A successful businessman

Playing the piano and the computer keyboard!

Today, Patrick works for big technology companies, helping them to find solutions to their business problems. His *invention*, the Delta-T Probe, is in the Science Museum in London and his Rubik's Cube book became the fastest selling book in history, selling 1.5 million copies in 1982.

Sergio Salvatore continues to write music, including online music. He also performs all over the world. In 2008 he recorded a new CD with Christos Rafalides, a famous vibraphonist*, called Dark Sand.

* A vibraphonist plays a vibraphone. This is a percussion instrument for jazz music.

Michelle Kwan is studying *International Affairs* at university. She's a writer and a TV star. She was the *voice* of the shop assistant in the film *Mulan II*. She's still skating and she's training hard for the next winter Olympics.

On the ice

Cool inventions

Match the headings with the inventions.

The Flying Car

Fresh Pizza Fast

Holographic TV

Travel Guitar

Pet GPS

1 You're really hungry and your pizza isn't here. You ordered it 30 minutes ago!

You need a Super Fast Pizza. This American company *designed* a *van* with a kitchen inside it. Their vans drive round and cook the pizzas when they *receive* an *order*. You order your pizza by phone or online and the message goes to a van near your street. The driver puts the pizza in the *oven* and arrives at your house 10 minutes later. And the pizza is still hot!

2 The Claro TV is made of glass and when you turn it off, you can't see it. The glass is a special glass that creates *holographic images*. It hasn't got any *wires* and there isn't a box round it, but there is a *projector* behind it. You get an amazingly clear, big picture. When you're watching this TV, you *feel like* you're inside the screen.

3 This car is called Transition. It's a car that *turns into* a plane! Just drive the Transition to the nearest airport, *press a button* and the *wings* open out from the sides of the car. Thirty seconds later, you're in a small aeroplane. It can fly at 193 kilometres per hour but it doesn't fly very high. It only flies 1.6 kilometres up in the sky.

... now it's a plane!

4 Have you got a dog that likes to run and doesn't come back? Do you sometimes lose your dog? Then, you need a RoamEO Location System. This is a dog *collar* and a *handheld receiver*. The system uses *GPS* technology. Satellites *track* your dog and send a signal every three seconds. The screen shows you where your dog is. You can also create a *virtual fence* – when your dog goes past the fence, an alarm sounds on the receiver.

5 If you play a big musical instrument, it's often difficult to take it on your travels with you. And it can be very difficult to take it on a plane. But if you play the guitar, there's now a *solution*. The Centrefold is a guitar that *folds in half*. You can put it into a small *rucksack* and carry it easily onto any plane or bus. You can even ride your bike with it on your back.

Word list Starter Unit and Unit 1

Starter

Classroom

bag (n) ....
board (n) ....
book (n) ....
chair (n) ....
desk (n) ....
dictionary (n) ....
door (n) ....
notebook (n) ....
pen (n) ....
pencil (n) ....
rubber (n) ....
ruler (n) ....
student (n) ....
teacher (n) ....
wall (n) ....
window (n) ....

Verbs

borrow (v) ....
help (v) ....
listen (v) ....
look (at) (v) ....
mean (v) ....
open (v) ....
sit down (v) ....
speak (v) ....
stand up (v) ....
study (v) ....
talk (v) ....
understand (v) ....
watch (v) ....
work (v) ....
write (v) ....

Unit 1

Family relationships

aunt (n) ....
brother (n) ....
children (n) ....
cousin (n) ....
daughter (n) ....
father (n) ....
grandfather (n) ....
grandmother (n) ....
grandparents (n) ....

mother (n) ....
nephew (n) ....
niece (n) ....
parents (n) ....
sister (n) ....
son (n) ....
uncle (n) ....

Appearance

dark/dark-haired (adj) ....
fair/fair-haired (adj) ....
fat (adj) ....
happy (adj) ....
old (adj) ....
red-haired (adj) ....
sad (adj) ....
short (adj) ....
tall (adj) ....
thin (adj) ....
young (adj) ....

Countries

Australia (n) ....
Austria (n) ....
Canada (n) ....
England (n) ....
France (n) ....
Germany (n) ....
Holland (n) ....
Hungary (n) ....
India (n) ....
Ireland (n) ....
Italy (n) ....
New Zealand (n) ....
Northern Ireland (n) ....
Poland (n) ....
Portugal (n) ....
Scotland (n) ....
Spain (n) ....
The United States (n) ....

Other words and expressions

address (n) ....
airport (n) ....
beautiful (adj) ....
because (conj) ....
between (prep) ....
big (adj) ....
birthday (n) ....

building (n) ....
capital city (n) ....
cold (adj) ....
date of birth (phr) ....
doctor (n) ....
east (n) ....
enormous (adj) ....
equator (n) ....
first name (n) ....
friend (n) ....
hospital (n) ....
hungry (adj) ....
impossible (adj) ....
latitude (n) ....
let's go (phr) ....
library (n) ....
longitude (n) ....
nice to meet you (phr) ....
north (n) ....
photo (n) ....
place (n) ....
scientist (n) ....
small (adj) ....
south (n) ....
suitcase (n) ....
surname (n) ....
telephone number (n) ....
travel card (n) ....
welcome (v) ....
west (n) ....

U1 Reading Explorer

coral reef (n) ....
grizzly bear (n) ....
kangaroo (n) ....
kiwi bird (n) ....
kiwi fruit (n) ....
koala bear (n) ....
polar bear (n) ....
seal (n) ....
sheep (n) ....
warrior (n) ....

Word list Unit 2

Possessions

camera (n) ....
car (n) ....
comic (n) ....
key (n) ....
mobile phone (n) ....
photo album (n) ....
purse (n) ....
toy (n) ....
umbrella (n) ....
watch (n) ....

Skills and abilities

climb (v) ....
cook (v) ....
copy a CD (v) ....
drive (v) ....
fly (v) ....
jump (v) ....
make (v) ....
move (v) ....
play the piano (phr) ....
send an email (phr) ....
speak Spanish (phr) ....
swim (v) ....
use the Internet (phr) ....

Months

January (n) ....
February (n) ....
March (n) ....
April (n) ....
May (n) ....
June (n) ....
July (n) ....
August (n) ....
September (n) ....
October (n) ....
November (n) ....
December (n) ....

Other words and expressions

across (prep) ....
act (v) ....
amazing (adj) ....
ammonite (n) ....
around (prep) ....
bed (n) ....

bedroom (n) ....
bite (n) ....
bring (v) ....
blind (adj) ....
cake (n) ....
change (v) ....
check (v) ....
clothes (n) ....
collection (n) ....
dance (v) ....
disabled (adj) ....
emergency services (n) ....
favourite (adj) ....
feet (n) ....
female (adj) ....
fossil (n) ....
go shopping (phr) ....
great (adj) ....
hero (n) ....
holiday (n) ....
human (n) ....
judge (n) ....
late (adj) ....
leg (n) ....
male (adj) ....
monkey (n) ....
mountain (n) ....
operate (v) ....
period (n) ....
poster (n) ....
ready (adj) ....
recognise (v) ....
record (n) ....
shape (n) ....
sing (v) ....
song (n) ....
snake (n) ....
tail (adj) ....
tortoise (n) ....
tree (n) ....
unusual (adj) ....
valuable (adj) ....
venom (n) ....
wait (v) ....
win (v) ....
wing (n) ....
world (n) ....

Ordinal numbers

first (adj) ....
second (adj) ....
third (adj) ....
fourth (adj) ....
fifth (adj) ....
sixth (adj) ....
seventh (adj) ....
eighth (adj) ....
ninth (adj) ....
tenth (adj) ....

U2 Reading Explorer

appetite (n) ....
bug (n) ....
chameleon (n) ....
cub (n) ....
energy (n) ....
hump (n) ....
leopard (n) ....
lizard (n) ....
mood (n) ....
patient (adj) ....
shoot out (phr) ....
speciality (n) ....
surroundings (n) ....
tail (n) ....
thirsty (adj) ....
tongue (n) ....

Word list Unit 3

School subjects

art (n) ....
biology (n) ....
chemistry (n) ....
English (n) ....
French (n) ....
geography (n) ....
history (n) ....
IT (n) ....
maths (n) ....
music (n) ....
PE (n) ....
physics (n) ....

Interests and activities

cycling (n) ....
dancing (n) ....
drawing (n) ....
painting (n) ....
fashion (n) ....
films (n) ....
language (n) ....
motorbike (n) ....
reading (n) ....
shopping (n) ....
singing (n) ....
sleeping (n) ....
sports (n) ....

Food and drink

apple (n) ....
banana (n) ....
bread (n) ....
cake (n) ....
cheese (n) ....
chicken (n) ....
chips (n) ....
chocolate (n) ....
doughnut (n) ....
fish (n) ....
fish and chips (phr) ....
ham (n) ....
ice cream (n) ....
lamb (n) ....
meat (n) ....
milk (n) ....
milkshake (n) ....

mushroom (n) ....
oil (n) ....
onion (n) ....
orange (n) ....
pasta (n) ....
potato (n) ....
rice (n) ....
salad (n) ....
sausage (n) ....
strawberry (n) ....
tomato (n) ....
tuna (n) ....
vegetable (n) ....
yoghurt (n) ....

Films

action (n) ....
actor (n) ....
adventure film (n) ....
the bad guy (phr) ....
director (n) ....
superhero (n) ....

Other words and expressions

ambition (n) ....
balanced diet (phr) ....
children (n pl) ....
chopstick (n) ....
designer (n) ....
different (adj) ....
double (adj) ....
guitar (n) ....
hamster (n) ....
hate (v) ....
healthy (adj) ....
husband (n) ....
include (v) ....
like (v) ....
love (v) ....
married (adj) ....
pets (n) ....
serve (v) ....
single (adj) ....
shorts (n pl) ....
smile (v) ....
touch (v) ....
triple (adj) ....

unhealthy (adj) ....
vegan (adj) ....
vegetarian (adj) ....
voice (n) ....
wife (n) ....

U3 Reading Explorer

add (v) ....
ant (n) ....
bake (v) ....
calcium (n) ....
caterpillar (n) ....
cricket (n) ....
dragonfly (n) ....
dreaming (n) ....
flour (n) ....
grasshopper (n) ....
honey (n) ....
iron (n) ....
larva (n) ....
mealworm (n) ....
oven (n) ....
pupa (n) ....
tray (n) ....
worm (n) ....

Word list Unit 4

Sports

athletics (n) ....
basketball (n) ....
boxing (n) ....
diving (n) ....
football (n) ....
gymnastics (n) ....
hockey (n) ....
running (n) ....
skating (n) ....
swimming (n) ....
skiing (n) ....
tennis (n) ....
volleyball (n) ....

Daily routine

arrive home (phr) ....
do homework (phr) ....
get dressed (phr) ....
get up (phr) ....
go to bed (phr) ....
have a bath (phr) ....
have breakfast (phr) ....
have dinner (phr) ....
have lunch (phr) ....
have a shower (phr) ....
leave the house (phr) ....

Time expressions

always (adv) ....
never (adv) ....
often (adv) ....
sometimes (adv) ....
usually (adv) ....

Other words and expressions

against (prep) ....
alarm clock (n) ....
arm (n) ....
author (n) ....
beach (n) ....
coach (n) ....
compete (v) ....
detention (n) ....
doubles (n) ....
difficult (adj) ....
early (adj) ....

fall (v) ....
football match (n) ....
fruit (n) ....
gym (n) ....
have fun (phr) ....
jump (v) ....
match (n) ....
make up (n) ....
opportunity (n) ....
pet rat (n) ....
preparation (n) ....
prize (n) ....
race (n) ....
spin (v) ....
summer (n) ....
team (n) ....
ticket (n) ....
training (n) ....
trophies (n pl) ....
until (prep) ....
winter (n) ....

Verbs

break (v) ....
do exercises (phr) ....
give (v) ....
go out (phr v) ....
hurt (v) ....
lose (v) ....
perform (v) ....
practise (v) ....
prepare (v) ....
relax (v) ....
support (v) ....
train (v) ....
walk (v) ....
win (v) ....

U4 Reading Explorer

bat (n) ....
board (n) ....
boat (n) ....
costume (n) ....
cylinder (n) ....
elevator (n) ....
helmet (n) ....
ledge (n) ....

life-jacket (n) ....
race (v) ....
ride (v) ....
rope (n) ....
route (n) ....
safe (adj) ....
waves (n) ....

Word list Unit 5

House and furniture

bath (n) ....

bathroom (n) ....

bed (n) ....

bedroom (n) ....

bin (n) ....

bottle (n) ....

cabin (n) ....

ceiling light (n) ....

chest of drawers (n) ....

cupboard (n) ....

dishwasher (n) ....

fridge (n) ....

garage (n) ....

garden (n) ....

kitchen (n) ....

living room (n) ....

microwave (n) ....

rechargeable
batteries (n pl) ....

rug (n) ....

shelves (n pl) ....

shower (n) ....

solar panel (n) ....

study (n) ....

table (n) ....

wardrobe (n) ....

washing machine (n) ....

Natural features

desert (n) ....

field (n) ....

ice (n) ....

lake (n) ....

mountain (n) ....

path (n) ....

river (n) ....

sea (n) ....

snow (n) ....

tree (n) ....

Other words and expressions

affect (v) ....

bear (n) ....

biscuit (n) ....

boat (n) ....

camera (n) ....

chimney (n) ....

count (v) ....

crocodile (n) ....

disappear (v) ....

dive (v) ....

egg (n) ....

entrance (n) ....

factory (n) ....

fire (n) ....

forest (n) ....

hit (v) ....

imagine (v) ....

increase (v) ....

Inuit (n) ....

joke (n) ....

level (n) ....

low-energy (adj) ....

melt (v) ....

middle (n) ....

neighbour (n) ....

newspaper (n) ....

paint (v) ....

parrot (n) ....

penguin (n) ....

push (v) ....

radio programme (n) ....

recycle (v) ....

result (n) ....

rise (v) ....

roof (n) ....

save (v) ....

shadow (n) ....

sunbed (n) ....

supper (n) ....

switch off (phr v) ....

teenager (n) ....

text message (n) ....

top (n) ....

towards (prep) ....

village (n) ....

webcam (n) ....

U5 Reading Explorer

attract (v) ....

beak (n) ....

call loudly (phr) ....

chick (n) ....

emperor penguin (n) ....

flipper (n) ....

from side to
side (phr) ....

mate (n) ....

nest (n) ....

steal (v) ....

stone (n) ....

up and down (phr) ....

Word list Unit 6

Clothes

boots (n) ....

cap (n) ....

coat (n) ....

dress (n) ....

gloves (n pl) ....

jacket (n) ....

jeans (n pl) ....

sandals (n pl) ....

shirt (n) ....

shoes (n pl) ....

skirt (n) ....

socks (n pl) ....

sunglasses (n pl) ....

sweatshirt (n) ....

trainers (n pl) ....

trousers (n pl) ....

T-shirt (n) ....

Places in a town

church (n) ....

cinema (n) ....

post office (n) ....

restaurant (n) ....

shop (n) ....

sports centre (n) ....

Other words and expressions

adult (n) ....

advice (n) ....

baggy (adj) ....

beads (n) ....

boring (adj) ....

breakfast (n) ....

change (money) (v) ....

choose (v) ....

coast (n) ....

comfortable (adj) ....

container (n) ....

destination (n) ....

dye (v) ....

easy (adj) ....

equipment (n) ....

exciting (adj) ....

fashionable (adj) ....

government (n) ....

hair (n) ....

hat (n) ....

insect (n) ....

key ring (n) ....

mug (n) ....

nice (adj) ....

postcard (n) ....

raise (v) ....

rubbish (n) ....

school trip (n) ....

sleeve (n) ....

stamp (n) ....

terrible (adj) ....

warm (adj) ....

water sports (n) ....

U6 Reading Explorer

amphitheatre (n) ....

ancient (adj) ....

architecture (n) ....

castle (n) ....

concrete (n) ....

dome (n) ....

emperor (n) ....

memory (n) ....

peninsula (n) ....

ruin (n) ....

sea level (n) ....

square (n) ....

statue (n) ....

stone (n) ....

temple (n) ....

tower (n) ....

valley (n) ....

wonder (n) ....

Word list Unit 7

Adjectives

bored (adj) ....
excited (adj) ....
happy (adj) ....
ill (adj) ....
nervous (adj) ....
tired (adj) ....

Irregular verbs

begin (v)   began (v) ....
buy (v)   bought (v) ....
come (v)   came (v) ....
drink (v)   drank (v) ....
eat (v)   ate (v) ....
give (v)   gave (v) ....
go (v)   went (v) ....
have (v)   had (v) ....
make (v)   made (v) ....
read (v)   read (v) ....
say (v)   said (v) ....
see (v)   saw (v) ....
take (v)   took (v) ....
win (v)   won (v) ....
write (v)   wrote (v) ....

Other words and expressions

at the weekend (phr) ....
barbecue (n) ....
be born (v) ....
burn (v) ....
celebrate (v) ....
celebration (n) ....
christening (n) ....
confused (adj) ....
congratulations (n pl) ....
delicious (adj) ....
difference (n) ....
discover (v) ....
divorce (n) ....
driving test (n) ....
edit (v) ....
gift (n) ....
good luck (phr) ....
heat (n) ....
I'd love to (phr) ....
imagination (n) ....
invitation (n) ....
kid (n) ....
meal (n) ....

meteor (n) ....
mind (n) ....
missing (adj) ....
Mother's Day (n) ....
New Year's Eve (n) ....
oxygen (n) ....
pass (v) ....
present (n) ....
primary school (n) ....
record (v) ....
reunite (v) ....
sandwich (n) ....
scared (adj) ....
See you there! (phr) ....
sky (n) ....
spaceship (n) ....
special effects (n pl) ....
sunrise (n) ....
thermometer (n) ....
together (adv) ....
tool (n) ....
toothache (n) ....
torch (n) ....
town (n) ....
twin (n) ....
useful (adj) ....
wedding (n) ....
wedding anniversary (n) ....
What's up? (phr) ....
worried (adj) ....
yesterday (n) ....

U7 Reading Explorer

combine (v) ....
compose (v) ....
cube (n) ....
jazz (n) ....
percussion (n) ....
pianist (n) ....
prodigy (n) ....

Word list Unit 8

Technology

computer (n)	....
keyboard (n)	....
mouse (n)	....
printer (n)	....
screen (n)	....
speakers (n pl)	....
webcam (n)	....

Adverbs

badly (adv)	....
carelessly (adv)	....
happily (adv)	....
loudly (adv)	....
quickly (adv)	....
quietly (adv)	....
slowly (adv)	....
well (adv)	....

Irregular verbs

feel (v)	felt (v)	....
find (v)	found (v)	....
forget (v)	forgot (v)	....
leave (v)	left (v)	....
lose (v)	lost (v)	....
put (v)	put (v)	....
sell (v)	sold (v)	....
send (v)	sent (v)	....
speak (v)	spoke (v)	....
steal (v)	stole (v)	....
stick (v)	stuck (v)	....
tell (v)	told (v)	....
think (v)	thought (v)	....
understand (v)	understood (v)	....

Other words and expressions

communications satellite (n)	....
axis (n)	....
believe (v)	....
bone (n)	....
connection (n)	....
crown (n)	....
deep (adj)	....
design (n)	....
develop (v)	....
discover (v)	....
gold (n)	....
Earth (n)	....

follow (v)	....
happen (v)	....
impact (n)	....
invent (v)	....
invention (n)	....
look for (phr v)	....
muscle (n)	....
planet (n)	....
plant (n)	....
receive (v)	....
return (v)	....
scales (n pl)	....
seed (n)	....
silver (n)	....
solar cells (n pl)	....
solar eclipse (n)	....
somebody (n)	....
space (n)	....
sticky (adj)	....
sun (n)	....
telescope (n)	....
universe (n)	....
Velcro (n)	....
weigh (v)	....
well (n)	....
windy (n)	....

U8 Reading Explorer

collar (n)	....
handheld receiver (n)	....
holographic (adj)	....
projector (n)	....
rucksack (n)	....
track (v)	....
virtual (adj)	....
wire (n)	....